THE **MINI** ROUGH GUIDE TO
BELGRADE

ROUGH
GUIDES

YOUR TAILOR-MADE TRIP
STARTS HERE

Tailor-made trips and unique adventures crafted by local experts

Rough Guides has been inspiring travellers for more than 35 years. Leave it to our local experts to create your perfect itinerary and book it at local rates.

Don't follow the crowd – find your own path.

HOW ROUGHGUIDES.COM/TRIPS WORKS

STEP 1 Pick your dream destination, tell us what you want and submit an enquiry.

STEP 2 Fill in a short form to tell your local expert about your dream trip and preferences.

STEP 3 Our local expert will craft your tailor-made itinerary. You'll be able to tweak and refine it until you're completely satisfied.

STEP 4 Book online with ease, pack your bags and enjoy the trip! Our local expert will be on hand 24/7 while you're on the road.

PLAN AND BOOK YOUR TRIP AT
ROUGHGUIDES.COM/TRIPS

HOW TO DOWNLOAD YOUR FREE EBOOK

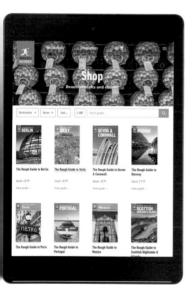

1. Visit **www.roughguides.com/free-ebook** or scan the **QR code** below

2. Enter the code **belgrade743**

3. Follow the simple step-by-step instructions

For troubleshooting contact: mail@roughguides.com

10 THINGS NOT TO MISS

1

4

5

2

6

3

7

A PERFECT DAY

9.30am

Brunch in Dorćol. Drinking coffee with friends is a ritual of daily life in the Western Balkans, so start as you mean to go on, caffeinating at a leisurely pace in the elegant Dorćol neighbourhood. French bistro-style *Pastis* and friendly *Red Bread* (see page 108) both have great breakfast options.

10.30am

Kalemegdan Fortress. Take in the commanding views of the point where the mighty Danube meets her tributary the Sava, and of the post-war utopian project, New Belgrade, beyond. Explore the meandering Kalemegdan complex, pausing at the tiny, gemlike Ružica Church – a microcosm of Serbian Orthodox design – and Ivan Meštrović's iconic 1928 *Victor* statue.

11.30am

Military Museum. Get to grips with Serbia's history of conflict. Unforgettable exhibits include the bloodstained garments of Yugoslav King Alexander Karadjordević, assassinated in France in 1934, and weapons captured from US soldiers during the NATO bombardment in 1999.

12.30pm

Exploring the Old Town. Head out of the Kalemegdan complex to St Michael's Cathedral, popping over the road to the beautiful Residence of Princess Ljubica to see how fashions changed over the nineteenth century as Serbia sought to assert its place among the European family of nations.

2pm

Lunchtime. Stroll down the central pedestrianized thoroughfare, Knez Mihailova, before refuelling at

IN BELGRADE

Supermarket Deli on picturesque Topličin Venac or Belgrade's most famous tavern, *Znak Pitanja* (Question Mark).

3pm

National Museum. Buff up on Serbian culture at the refurbished National Museum on the city's main square, Trg Republike, pausing en route to admire Prince Mihailo's horse.

4pm

Sugar rush. Fend off that mid-afternoon energy slump with artisanal gelato from *Bacio* in Dorćol, afternoon tea at the iconic *Hotel Moskva* on Terazije or picture-perfect creations at *Mandarina* cake shop in the Old Town.

5.30pm

Bar-hopping. While away an hour or two exploring Belgrade's characterful drinking dens, such as the *World Travellers' Club* (see page 89) or *Blaznavac* (see page 87).

8pm

Sample national cuisine. Tackle a *karadjordje schnitzel* on Skadarska In homage to Serbia's national hero while listening to the soulful strains of Serbian folk song, or choose instead the cultured surrounds of the venerable *Writers' Club*, erstwhile haunt of the Yugoslav literati.

10pm

Cetinjska complex. Sample local craft beers and live music at the buzzy *Cetinjska* complex, a favourite of Belgrade's young hipster creatives, set in a former brewery just around the corner from Skadarlija.

CONTENTS

HIGHLIGHTS

A NOTE TO READERS

At Rough Guides, we always strive to bring you the most up-to-date information. This book was produced during a period of continuing uncertainty caused by the Covid-19 pandemic, so please note that content is more subject to change than usual. We recommend checking the latest restrictions and official guidance.

OVERVIEW

Serbia's capital city, Belgrade has an alchemy all of its own, some-how combining grit and glitz, post-Communist greyscale with a Southern European zest for life. In recent years, burgeoning num-bers of visitors have been captivated by what lies beneath the scuffed facades and ubiquitous graffiti: the city's unbridled energy, off-beat creativity, unapologetic self-confidence and boundless determination to have a good time.

Belgrade is home to around 1.5 million people, making it the biggest city by some margin in a country of just over 8 million (excluding Kosovo). Serbia borders Hungary to the north, Croatia, Montenegro and Bosnia-Herzegovina to the west, Bulgaria and Romania to the east, and to the south, the Republic of Northern Macedonia and its former province, Kosovo. A would-be European Union member state, Serbia also cultivates close political and cultural ties with Russia. Its borders remain disputed fol-lowing Kosovo's declaration of independence in 2008, and talks continue to try to resolve these issues.

It's customary to observe, by way of preamble, that Belgrade doesn't quite live up to its name – the White City (*beli grad*). But

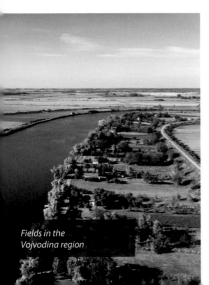
Fields in the Vojvodina region

its reputation for grit has become, increasingly, a draw for visitors seeking out a taste of Yugonostalgia and a flavour of the vanished Communist East. Belgrade by day has a generous sprinkling of cultural and historical gems to offer, but by night it vibes to a long-established clubbing scene, and even enjoys a freshly minted reputation as a hipsters' paradise; happen on the right alternative spots, and you can scarcely move for manbuns and craft beer.

GEOGRAPHY

Belgrade lies at the juncture between two distinct landscapes: the Pannonian plain stretching across the flat Vojvodina region to the north up to the border with Hungary – and to the south, the hills and mountains of the Balkans. It sits squarely at the confluence of two rivers – the Danube, Europe's second-largest river after the Volga, and its tributary the Sava. The city boundaries straddle the Sava: the Old Town and its surrounds unfurling from the east bank and, on the west bank, the Communist-era New Belgrade development and picturesque Zemun.

With around 200km (125 miles) of riverbank running through the city, the river shapes and defines the city's life and topography. Its location on the Danube (or *Dunav*) has been for centuries central to Belgrade's strategic importance, both for trade and politics, linking it to the web of trading nations along the river's course. From the early eighteenth to the early twentieth centuries, the Danube and Sava jointly formed a political and cultural frontline between the Ottoman and Austro-Hungarian empires which occupied Belgrade and Zemun, respectively.

HISTORY

From distant medieval kingdoms to the wars of the 1990s, an awareness of the past pulses through Serbian culture and politics. As travel writer Rebecca West wrote in *Black Lamb and Grey Falcon*,

Archduke Franz Ferdinand

her classic narrative of her travels through Yugoslavia in the late 1930s: "I had come to Yugoslavia to see what history meant in flesh and blood".

If in the late nineteenth century, Belgrade was to most European statesmen an obscure corner of 'Turkey in Europe' to be horse-traded by competing Great Powers, in the twentieth century it blazed its way into wider consciousness with the assassination of Archduke Franz Ferdinand that triggered World War I (see page 22). Perceptions of Serbia in the West would shift significantly over the twentieth century: in World War I, Serbia was seen as a plucky little victim of Austrian aggression, but it ended the century under UN sanctions, widely condemned as an aggressor by the international community, and became in 1999 the only European country ever to be bombed by NATO.

In between, Belgrade was the political heart of two Yugoslavias: first the interwar Kingdom, and later the post-war Communist state founded in 1945. Right across the twentieth century, the decisions made in Belgrade affected citizens from Slovenia to Sarajevo, from Croatia's Adriatic coastline to the rugged mountains of Kosovo and Macedonia. Under the leadership of Josip Broz (Tito), Yugoslavia became a leading global player, steering a delicate course between East and West in the Cold War years. Tito's regime brought ordinary Yugoslavs peace, relative prosperity and excellent visa-free travel opportunities – something many in Serbia today miss.

Over the 1990s, the federal Yugoslav state splintered into its constituent parts, bringing war and untold suffering to millions. No visitor can leave Belgrade without a sense of the way the war's legacy still reverberates in politics and social attitudes, from the decision to leave untouched the government buildings ripped apart by NATO airstrikes (see page 61) to Serbia's geopolitical balancing-act between Russia and the West (see page 66).

ARCHITECTURE

Today's built environment accurately reflects Serbia's tumultuous twentieth century. It was bombed four times over the century – by Austria-Hungary in 1914, by both Axis powers (1941) and Allies (1944) during World War II and, most recently, by NATO (1999). The city wears its scars with a kind of defiant pride, leaving certain key sites of NATO bombing unrepaired more than twenty years on (see page 63). And with Belgrade's high levels of air pollution – among

A TWO-HEADED LANGUAGE

Uniquely among Balkan countries, Serbia's language (like the eagle on its flag) looks both east and west, using both Cyrillic and Latin scripts. The Cyrillic version is Serbia's official language and is used in government administration. The Serbian Cyrillic alphabet was developed by linguist Vuk Karadžić in 1814, an important marker of national identity around the time of the First Serbian Uprising, but is deemed increasingly under threat as the internet and globalization have made the Latin alphabet (latinica) increasingly the default. In 2018, the Ministry of Culture announced new measures to preserve Serbian Cyrillic ('the language and script are what we are').

Europe's worst – even the most pristine new buildings are prone to tarnish quickly.

Considering its duration, little survives of the Ottoman period in Belgrade: notable exceptions are the Bajrakli mosque (see page 54) and the grand residences of Prince Miloš and Princess Ljubica (see pages 75 and 48). At that time, the majority of buildings were wooden, single-storey, and prone to fire damage. The Hapsburg administration which took Belgrade over from the Ottomans in 1717–39 snuck in Baroque touches and converted mosques into churches.

It was only with the withdrawal of Ottoman troops from its territory in 1867, however, that Serbia launched a concerted rebuilding programme to mark its emergence as a player on the European stage. Belgrade's first urban planner, Emilijan Josimović,

The Residence of Prince Miloš, a traditional Balkan-style house

was on a mission to modernize the city. The 1880s and 1890s brought the arrival of railway links to Europe, electrical lighting, waterworks, and horse-drawn trams: in short, all the trappings of modernity.

In the interwar Kingdom of Yugoslavia, the Karadjordjević dynasty oversaw the building of remarkable architecture, notably the romantic nationalist Royal Palace at Dedinje. In post-war Communist Yugoslavia, architecture took a Brutalist turn, with monumental pieces of civic and residential design such as the 1977–80 Genex Tower, the 1969 Hotel Yugoslavia and the 1959 Palace of Serbia, studding the landscape of the *blokovi* (residential tower blocks) on the left bank of the Sava.

TOURIST BOOM

Visitor numbers to Belgrade have climbed fast in more recent years, with tourists from China, Turkey and Russia flocking to the city, as well as increased numbers of visitors from Western Europe and the US. The city has made concerted efforts to shake off the legacy of conflict and international isolation, with revamps of the city centre, renovations of all the major museums, and new flight routes opening up from national carrier Air Serbia. You can expect a generally friendly welcome, with the younger generation in particular speaking very good English.

That said, for many visitors, part of the appeal is the sense that Serbia is a safe but still slightly edgy destination; a manageably adventurous option just a short hop from Western Europe. Although the scars of conflict are still etched across the city's streets, and in some respects actively promoted by the authorities, it's worth stressing that post-conflict tourism isn't particularly welcomed by all residents, and that in conversation, you would do best to steer clear of sensitive topics (Kosovo and the wars of the former Yugoslavia).

HISTORY AND CULTURE

Even as a casual visitor, you will find that Serbian history is ever-present in what you see, hear and are told in Belgrade. Here as across the Western Balkans, the telling and interpretation of the recent past remains heavily contested and deeply split along ethnic lines. To the extent that the conflicts of the 1990s are referred to, the emphasis is typically on the damage caused by the 1999 NATO bombing of Belgrade, and the phrase 'NATO aggression' is one you are likely to hear from tour guides. The Milošević years, the NATO bombing and the current status of Kosovo remain topics to handle with extreme care.

BEGINNINGS

The majority of the lands now known as the Balkans were conquered by the Roman Empire in the first century AD. At that time, the populations living in this corner of Southeastern Europe were a diverse mix, including Greeks, Thracians, Dardanians and Illyrians. Some historians argue that as many as eighteen Roman emperors were born on the territory of modern-day Serbia. Only in the sixth century did Slavonic-speaking peoples – or Slavs – begin to migrate into the Balkans. They settled in the seventh century and by the mid-ninth century, the group known as the Serbs were settled around Raška, in southern Serbia.

THE MEDIEVAL PERIOD

Various Serbian principalities (or kingdoms) arose in the medieval period, but the most politically important by far was Stefan Nemanja's dynasty, founded in Raška in the 1160s. The Nemanjić dynasty lasted for 200 years and became a major military force in the region, taking most of today's Albania and Macedonia. The

Vestiges of NATO bombing

Nemanjić dynasty later became a vital reference point for Serbian independence movements, seen as a golden age in which Serbian identity was forged. The kingdom declined and shrank rapidly in the fourteenth century under Stefan Uros V ('the Weak'), who died in 1371.

OTTOMAN CONQUEST

The 1371 Battle of Maritsa marked the arrival of a new dominant political force in the region: the Ottomans. Belgrade resisted Ottoman forces in the siege of 1456, when the Hungarian Janos Hunyadi led the city's defence; but in 1521 it succumbed to the armies of Sultan Suleiman the Magnificent. Far and away the most famous battle in the history of the Ottoman conquest of Serbia, however, is the Battle of Kosovo Polje (also known as the Field of Blackbirds) on 28 June 1389. The date is also known in Serbia as St Vitus' Day, or Vidovdan, and has a sacral importance to Serbs. The

Karadjordje statue

Serbian army was led by Prince Lazar Hrebeljanovic (often called Tsar Lazar, although he was a *knez* or prince, not an emperor); the Ottomans were led into battle by Sultan Murad I. Both Lazar and Sultan Murad died – the Sultan stabbed to death in his tent by Serbian knight Miloš Obilić – and although the battle was technically a draw, it was remembered as a Serbian defeat.

BETWEEN TWO EMPIRES

Under Ottoman rule, Kalemegdan Fortress became a garrison and the seat of the *pasha* or military governor, ruling on the Sultan's behalf. The residents of Belgrade were predominantly ethnically Turkish administrators, merchants and military; Serbs moved out into the villages, where Muslim landlords ruled over Christian peasantry.

Throughout the late seventeenth and eighteenth centuries Belgrade ricocheted back and forth between the two dominant regional powers, the Austro-Hungarian Hapsburg Empire and the Ottoman Empire. As the competing armies surged across central and southeastern Europe between Vienna and Istanbul, the Austro-Hungarians captured Belgrade three times between 1688 and 1791, and held it for more than 20 years from 1717–39, but each time Belgrade was eventually retaken by the Ottomans. Meanwhile, Serbian nationalism began to develop in earnest, inspiring the first national uprisings.

RISE OF NATIONALISM

In the First Serbian Uprising (1804–13), the *hajduks* (liberation fighters) led by Karadjordje launched a guerrilla rebellion against Ottoman rule (see box), sparked by an incident in which up to 150

KARADJORDJE AND HIS HAJDUKS

One of the most colourful figures in Serbian history is Djordje Petrović, known as Karadjordje or 'Black George' (1752–1817). A pig trader by background, he led the First Serbian Uprising of 1804–13, liberating the entire Belgrade *pashalik* (province) from the Ottomans. His armies were made up of *hajduks*, guerrillas or freedom fighters operating in small bands. Although the Ottomans eventually quashed the rebellion, it is claimed that Napoleon Bonaparte – his contemporary – praised Karadjordje's military achievements in light of his limited resources. In 1817, Karadjordje returned from exile abroad, but Miloš Obrenović – the rebels' leader in the Second Uprising of 1815, and a more cautious character – dispatched agents to assassinate Karadjordje. Killed with a *yatagan* (short Ottoman sabre), his head was skinned, stuffed and sent to the Sultan. His heirs founded one of Serbia's two rival royal dynasties. He is commemorated in the form of a striking statue by St Sava's Church (see page 66), and an imposing breaded sausage (see page 102).

The Double-headed Eagle

One of the few issues on which all Serbia's rival royal dynasties could agree was the proper royal logo to use: the double-headed eagle was adopted under the Nemanjić dynasty in the fourteenth century and used by both the Karadjordje and the Obrenović dynasties in the nineteenth.

Serbian nobles were executed by the Janissaries (elite troops, increasingly operating independently of the Sublime Porte in Istanbul). The Second Serbian Uprising followed hot on its heels in 1815–17, this time led by Miloš Obrenović.

EDGING TOWARDS INDEPENDENCE

Over the nineteenth century, Serbia gradually gained in autonomy as the increasingly weakened Ottoman Empire came under ever-growing pressure from a combination of armed Serbian rebels, savvy Serbian political operators and Great Powers willing to sponsor Serbia's cause.

In 1830, a decree from the Sultan (*hatti-sherif*) granted Serbia a semi-autonomous status within the Ottoman Empire, and the right for Serbian leader Miloš Obrenović to bear the hereditary title of prince (*knez*). The Ottoman army remained, however, still very much a presence, in six forts across Serbia, including Kalemegdan. In 1867 the Ottomans finally handed over Belgrade Fortress and the other five fortresses they held. At the Congress of Berlin in 1878, Serbia's de facto independence was recognized *de jure* by the Great Powers.

Meanwhile at home, political power alternated between two rival royal dynasties: the Karadjordjes and the Obrenovićs. The animosity between the two was fierce, dating back to the murder of Karadjordje by Obrenović's agents in 1817 (see box, page 19). In 1903, the last Obrenović king, Alexander, and his spectacularly unpopular older wife, Draga Mašin, were murdered in a military conspiracy known as the May Coup, their bodies thrown unceremoniously off the palace balcony. All royals since that date (including those now resident at the Royal Palaces in Dedinje) have been Karadjordjevićs.

FIRST AND SECOND BALKAN WARS

In the First Balkan War of 1912, Serbia teamed up with Montenegro, Bulgaria and Greece to drive the Ottomans out of the region. The campaign was a stunning success in dismembering the now weak and tottering 'sick man of Europe', and Serbia fulfilled one key territorial ambition in regaining control of Kosovo to the south, seen as its spiritual heartland. However, Balkan unity soon disintegrated, and in 1913 the Bulgarians launched the Second Balkan War, attacking their former allies to seek to increase their own

Serbian flags flying proudly

SA OVOG MJESTA 28 JUNA 1914 GODINE
GAVRILO PRINCIP JE IZVRŠIO ATENTAT NA
AUSTROUGARSKOG PRESTOLONASLJEDNIKA
FRANCA FERDINANDA I NJEGOVU SUPRUGU
SOFIJU

FROM THIS PLACE ON 28 JUNE 1914
GAVRILO PRINCIP ASSASSINATED THE HEIR
TO THE AUSTRO-HUNGARIAN THRONE
FRANZ FERDINAND AND HIS WIFE SOFIA

*Plaque in Sarajevo where Archduke
Franz Ferdinand was assassinated*

gains. The outcome went against Bulgaria, and Serbia on the cusp
of World War I had almost doubled its size.

WORLD WAR I

On 28 June 1914, Bosnian Serb nationalist Gavrilo Princip fired
the shot that triggered World War I, killing the Austro-Hungarian
Archduke Franz Ferdinand and his wife Sophie on a street corner
in Sarajevo. Despite the fact that the group which armed and supported Princip and his comrades (a nationalist secret society called
Unity or Death, also known as the Black Hand) was not allied to the
Serbian Government, and the Serbian Government had no knowl-
edge of the plot, the Austro-Hungarians took the assassination as
a pretext to declare war on Serbia.

Belgrade was shelled by the Austrians from their base in Zemun
as early as summer 1914, and completely occupied after a com-
bined Austro-Hungarian, German and Bulgarian assault in October

1915. The Serbs suffered an enormous human cost in the war, with the highest number of casualties proportional to the population of any country. It is estimated that the Balkan Wars and World War I jointly killed a quarter of the total population and two-thirds of men aged between 15 and 55.

THE INTERWAR YEARS

The Kingdom of Serbs, Croats and Slovenes was formed on 1 December 1918, a constitutional monarchy under the (Serbian) Karadjordjević dynasty. The new Kingdom was inherently unstable due to tensions between Serbs (the largest single population) and Croats (who saw this as a 'greater Serbia' project). Tensions came to a head in 1928, when a Montenegrin member of parliament opened fire in the Parliament Building, killing two fellow (Croat) members of

GAVRILO PRINCIP

Gavrilo Princip was the nineteen-year-old Bosnian Serb who assassinated Austria-Hungary's Archduke Franz Ferdinand on a street corner in Sarajevo on 28 June 1914. The date of the official visit was poorly chosen by the occupying imperial power – 28 June was remembered by all Serbs as the date of their national humiliation at the 1389 Battle of Kosovo. Born in Bosnia, it was during his time in Belgrade that Princip began to mix with political radicals, spending countless hours in the spring of 1914 with his two co-conspirators in down-at-heel cafés in the Zeleni Venac area, or Green Wreath Square (now the city's main fruit and veg market). He became determined to drive the Austro-Hungarians out of Bosnia and the wider 'south Slav' region. In his trial, Princip said: "I am a Yugoslav nationalist, aiming for the unification of all Yugoslavs, and I do not care what form of state, but it must be free from Austria."

The Nazi occupation of Belgrade

the legislature. The political crisis that followed saw riots in Zagreb, and in a bid to contain the fissiparous elements of his young kingdom, King Alexander Karadjordjević abolished parliament and made himself absolute ruler. As a symbolic move to promote unity, he also changed the name of the state to the Kingdom of Yugoslavia in 1929. But the forces for nationalism and separation were in the ascendant: King Alexander was assassinated in 1934 during a state visit to Marseille, alongside the French Foreign Minister, by a Macedonian assassin linked to the extreme Croat nationalist *Ustaša* party ('Uprising', led by Ante Pavelić). He was succeeded by his 11-year-old son Peter, with Alexander's cousin, Prince Paul, acting as regent.

WORLD WAR II

In March 1941, the government of Prince Paul signed a pact with the Nazis and the Axis powers. Two days later the government was overthrown in a popular coup, just as Hitler launched

Operation Punishment – the bombing of Yugoslavia. The Kingdom of Yugoslavia was carved up, with 'rump' Serbia placed under a Nazi client regime, the so-called 'Government of National Salvation' headed by former Yugoslav Minister of War, General Milan Nedić. The Independent State of Croatia (or NDH) was headed by the extreme Croatian nationalist Ante Pavelić, also a Nazi puppet regime. Pavelić's Ustaše regime persecuted Serbs ruthlessly, setting up concentration camps including Jasenovac, where an estimated 80,000–100,000 people were killed.

Two major resistance movements emerged during the war years, thriving in Yugoslavia's mountainous and forested terrain: the 'Četnik' resistance under the helm of Draža Mihailović, which supported the return of the Yugoslav royals (who were then in exile in London), and the Communist Partisans under the leadership of Josip Broz (Tito). Over time, the Četniks and Partisans increasingly fought each other, resulting in what was in effect a three-way civil war in places between Četniks, Partisans and Ustaše, with villages and ordinary people caught in the crossfire. It is estimated that in total one million people died in wartime Yugoslavia, of a population of sixteen million, and that half of those killed were Serbs.

AMONG THE PARTISANS

Winston Churchill's envoy, Fitzroy Maclean, was parachuted into Yugoslavia in 1943 to establish whether the Allies should support the Partisans. In his 1949 memoir, *Eastern Approaches*, Maclean wrote: "the Partisans were not dull people to live among. They would not have been Jugoslavs if they had been. Their innate turbulence, their natural independence, their deep-seated sense of the dramatic kept bubbling up in a number of unexpected ways … To what had started as a war they gave the character of a revolution."

A British Special Operations Executive (SOE) mission to Yugoslavia in 1943, led by Fitzroy Maclean, established that the Partisans held the initiative on the ground and had the best chance of both beating the Nazis and establishing a government that could command popular support after the war. The Allies therefore decide to arm and support the Partisans. Tito's Partisans liberated Belgrade from Nazi occupation on 20 October 1944.

POST-WAR YUGOSLAVIA

The new Socialist Federal Republic of Yugoslavia, founded in November 1945, had six constituent republics (Serbia, Croatia, Slovenia, Bosnia-Herzegovina, Macedonia and Montenegro) and two autonomous provinces (Kosovo and Vojvodina). It took as its slogan *bratsvo i jedinstvo:* brotherhood and unity, thus explicitly recognizing the differentness of its component nations. In the post-war years, statistics on those killed on all sides during World War II were deliberately not collected, in an attempt to build harmony across communities.

Yugoslavia enjoyed a unique position both within Eastern Europe and on the global stage: after the break with Stalin's Soviet Union in 1948, Tito steered a course between East and West, securing significant western financial support. In 1961 he founded a powerful bloc of largely post-colonial African and Asian nations, the non-aligned movement (NAM). In the early 1970s, national questions resurfaced in 'the Croatian Spring'; in 1974 the Yugoslav constitution was reformed, thereby increasing the decentralization of power.

In 1980, Tito's death marked the beginning of the end for Yugoslavia. The slogan "Even after Tito – Tito" was adopted to try to resume business as usual, but without a single uniting figurehead, ethnic tensions increased. The political and economic situation began to falter, with rampant inflation and the rise of organized

crime. In 1989, Serbian nationalist Slobodan Milošević assumed the Presidency of (the Yugoslav Republic of) Serbia.

THE BREAK-UP OF YUGOSLAVIA

The first multi-party elections for over half a century were held in Yugoslavia in 1990. Ethno-nationalist parties won in most places, amid mounting tensions between the constituent republics. Croatia and Slovenia pressed for greater decentralization, but Serbia had a strong interest in holding the federation together – both because Serbs had always been the dominant political force in Yugoslavia, and because of the large pockets of ethnically Serb communities scattered across the other republics. The Yugoslav National Army (JNA) in effect became the army of the Federal Republic of Yugoslavia (the new entity created in 1992, made up of Serbia and Montenegro).

On 25 June 1991, the parliaments of Slovenia and Croatia declared independence. The JNA was deployed to the affected borders. In Slovenia, the more straightforward case as it was eth-nically homogeneous, the 'Ten-Day War' took place, ending on 7 July 1991 with the JNA's retreat.

In Croatia, the ethnic Serb minority rejected the authority of the newly proclaimed Croatian state. Croatian Serbs – supported by Serbia and the JNA – declared an independent Serb state, the so-called 'Republic of Krajina'. In autumn 1991, Serb forces destroyed the city of Vukovar and shelled the historic city of Dubrovnik. In April 1992, with conflict still raging in Croatia, war broke out in Bosnia-Herzegovina, pitting Bosnian Muslims and Croats against Bosnian Serbs, who founded the self-declared breakaway territory of Republika Srpska. The Bosnian Serb army's siege of Sarajevo lasted for over three years. In August 1995, NATO launched air-strikes on the Bosnian Serbs, forcing them to the negotiating

The damage of NATO bombing on the southern Serbian town of Aleksinac

Serbia and Kosovo shaking hands at the 2013 Brussels Agreement

table. The conflicts in both Croatia and Bosnia ended in the autumn of 1995.

WAR IN KOSOVO

The twentieth century ended with the final conflict to convulse the entities of the former Yugoslavia. In 1998, following years of passive resistance under the Kosovar Albanian leader Ibrahim Rugova, the Kosovo Liberation Army (KLA; in Albanian, UÇK), a guerrilla movement seeking independence, began a sustained campaign against Serbian rule. A JNA military offensive in Kosovo displaced 250,000 Kosovar Albanians from their homes. In spring 1999, NATO intervened (without a UN Security Council mandate) to save lives and stop the ethnic cleansing, fearing another Srebrenica. In October 2000, Slobodan Milošević (president of the Federal Republic of Yugoslavia – the union of Serbia and Montenegro) was overthrown by popular protests in Belgrade.

Following the Kosovo war, the International Criminal Tribunal for the former Yugoslavia (ICTY) at The Hague put Slobodan Milošević in the dock, facing 66 counts of war crimes, including genocide; he died in pre-trial detention in 2006. The ICTY found that in July 1992, the Bosnian Serb army committed genocide in Srebrenica, killing up to 8,000 Bosnian Muslim men and boys. Both Ratko Mladić, head of the Bosnian Serb army, and Radovan Karadžić, leader of Republika Srpska, have been found guilty of genocide and crimes against humanity, and sentenced to life imprisonment.

SERBIA STANDS ALONE

In 2006, the state union between the remaining two republics of the former Yugoslavia, Serbia and Montenegro, was amicably dissolved. Under direct UN administration, Kosovo's status was left unresolved until February 2008 when the Kosovan government unilaterally declared independence. Kosovo has been recognized as an independent country by around half the UN's member states, with the UK and US key backers, but Serbia continues to consider Kosovo a part of its sovereign territory. A number of countries that initially recognized Kosovo have withdrawn recognition.

TOWARDS EUROPE?

Economically, the situation in Serbia can be challenging, with youth unemployment reaching 33 percent in 2021 and income inequality higher than in any EU country. Serbia is the biggest recipient of EU aid in the Western Balkans, and joining the EU is the government's top foreign policy priority. Relations with Kosovo remain the biggest stumbling-block. In 2013, Serbia and Kosovo reached the EU-brokered Brussels Agreement, aiming to dismantle the parallel institutions operating in Kosovo's Serb-majority areas. In 2020 Serbia and Kosovo agreed to normalize economic relations, and progress slowly continues.

IMPORTANT DATES

3rd century BC Celtic settlement Singidunum founded on the Danube.
6–7th centuries AD Slavic peoples arrive in South Slav lands.
9–11th centuries Occupied by Bulgarian, Hungarian, Byzantine kingdoms.
1284 Belgrade under Serbian control for the first time.
1389 Battle of Kosovo Polje.
1521 Belgrade falls to the Ottomans.
1804–13 First Serbian Uprising.
1815–17 Second Serbian Uprising.
1841 Belgrade declared capital of Serbia, now a semi-autonomous principality.
1867 Ottoman Empire withdraws its troops from Serbian territory.
1878 Serbia recognized as an independent state at Congress of Berlin.
1882 Serbia becomes a kingdom, instead of a principality.
1912–13 First Balkan War.
1913 Second Balkan War.
1914 Gavrilo Princip assassinates Archduke Franz Ferdinand; start of WWI.
1918 Formation of Kingdom of Serbs, Croats and Slovenes.
1929 King Alexander dissolves Parliament; declares Kingdom of Yugoslavia.
1934 King Alexander assassinated in Marseille.
1941 Nazi bombardment of Belgrade; client regime headed by Milan Nedić.
1944 Allied bombardment of Belgrade.
1945 Belgrade liberated; founding of Socialist Federal Republic of Yugoslavia.
1991–95 War in Slovenia, Croatia and Bosnia as Yugoslavia disintegrates.
1998–99 Kosovo War.
1999 NATO bombing campaign. Serbian forces withdraw from Kosovo.
2000 Milošević overthrown by popular protests.
2006 Dissolution of the State Union between Serbia and Montenegro.
2008 Kosovo declares independence.
2013 Signature of Brussels Agreement to normalize relations with Kosovo.
2014 Serbia's EU accession negotiations begin.
2016–17 Radovan Karadžić and Ratko Mladić found guilty of genocide and crimes against humanity at The Hague.
2020 Covid-19 pandemic spreads throughout the world.

The striking Ada Bridge

OUT AND ABOUT

Belgrade's essential attractions are concentrated largely within the Old Town, or *Stari Grad*. This historic core can be considered to include the web of streets fanning out from Kalemegdan Fortress, anchored to the south by Brankov bridge (Brankov most), to the west by the Sava river and to the north by the outer fringes of the Dorćol quarter. Offering most of historical and cultural interest are Knez Mihailova and the streets that branch off it, Trg Republike and Studentski Trg, the three crescents (Topličin venac, Kosančićev venac and Obilićev venac), Skadarlija and Dorćol. If you're on a flying visit, don't miss the three quintessential Belgrade experiences handily concentrated in this area: taking in the vistas from Kalemegdan Fortress, tucking into a grilled meat lunch in Skadarlija and bar-hopping in Dorćol.

Beyond the Old Town, a clutch of attractions lies close to busy Bulevar kralja Aleksandra: the Parliament Building (Skupština Srbije), Tašmajdan Park and St Mark's Church. Following a different route out of the city centre, it is a 20-minute walk along Terazije and Kralja Milana to the Vračar area, which rivals Dorćol as a hub of Belgrade's thriving café culture and is home to the monumental St Sava's Church.

Any visitor with a day or two more to spare should venture further afield to take in the more dispersed charms of the city, which

What's in a Name?

The Serbian for street is *ulica*, often shortened to 'ul.'; a boulevard is '*bulevar*', a square '*trg*' and a crescent '*venac*'. Streets are often referred to without giving '*ulica*'; that convention is followed here. Many streets are named after Serbian royals: '*knez*' means prince and '*kralja*', king.

Old Town cityscape

are clustered in two main areas: the wide-open green spaces and seemingly endless riverbanks threading through New Belgrade and Zemun on the Sava's left bank; and Dedinje's pair of fascinating historical sites: the Royal Palaces and the Museum of Yugoslavia.

OLD TOWN (STARI GRAD)

Belgrade's Old Town has no clearly defined boundaries, but can be taken to include Kalemegdan Fortress; the central grid of streets surrounding pedestrianized Kneza Mihailova, which ends at Trg Republike (Republic Square); pretty Topličin venac and Kosančićev venac in the area sometimes fondly called Belgrade's Montmartre; trendy Dorćol; and the cobblestoned streets of the former bohemian quarter Skadarlija. The Old Town is best explored on foot; helpful new public maps in English have been set up around the Old Town and Vračar to help visitors orientate themselves and easily find tourist attractions.

KALEMEGDAN FORTRESS COMPLEX

The imposing **Kalemegdan Fortress ❶**, and the verdant park that surrounds it, remains the natural starting point for any visitor looking to get a sense of the geography and history of Belgrade. Splendidly sited on an exposed nub of land overlooking the confluence of the Sava and Danube rivers, the grand fortress dominates the city's skyline. It is easy to understand why this lofty spot was favoured for defensive purposes by a succession of occupying forces over the centuries, from the Romans to the Ottomans and Austro-Hungarians.

Kalemegdan was the stronghold of Ottoman power in Serbia from the final Ottoman conquest of Belgrade in 1521 until the late nineteenth century, and its name derives from Turkish: *kale* for fortress and *meydan* for battlefield. The complex system of inner and outer walls and gates was added during a short-lived Austrian occupation in the early eighteenth century.

The fortress finally passed permanently into Serbian hands in a ceremony in April 1867 when the last Ottoman pasha or military governor, Ali Reza Pasha, handed the keys over to Serbia's Prince Mihailo Obrenović.

The conquest of Belgrade by the Ottomans, 1521

The Victor statue inside the Kalemegdan Fortress

KALEMEGDAN PARK

The lush park wrapping around the fortress – reached by crossing busy Pariska from the northern end of Knez Mihailova – is one of the city's most pleasant, dotted with neat topiary and sweet-scented rose bushes. Nearing the fortress, the eye is immediately drawn to the sinuous contours of the **Monument of Gratitude to France** ❷. Unveiled on Armistice Day (11 November) in 1930, this was the work of esteemed Croatian (and Yugoslav) sculptor Ivan Meštrović, who also created the iconic *Victor* statue inside the fortress walls.

The front of the pedestal bears the inscription '*À la France*', the back the words (in Cyrillic), '*Let us love France as she loved us*'. The reference is to staunch French support for Serbia during World War I, both military (the joint Franco-Serbian offensive in 1916–17 in the Salonika campaign) and humanitarian (France welcomed 3,000 Serbian refugee children displaced by the war).

Over the years, this monument has reflected the ups and downs of Serbian-French relations. During the 1999 NATO bombings, in which France took part, it was covered by activists with a black veil. In 2018, the words '*À la France*' were struck through in black paint in protest at a diplomatic incident in which Serbian President Alexander Vučić was placed in an obscure third-row seat during World War I commemorations in Paris attended by European leaders.

Facing the monument, set back on at Pariska 11 – the main road you cross from Knez Mihailova to reach Kalemegdan Park – is the splendid 1935 Art Deco French Embassy. Topped with bronze statues of *liberté*, *égalité* and *fraternité*, the embassy stakes a fair claim to the accolade of Belgrade's most classically beautiful building. Gain the best view of it by bearing left on the footpath on entering the park, to walk parallel with Pariska.

WITHIN THE FORTRESS WALLS

To enter the fortress proper from the surrounding park, pass behind the Monument of Gratitude to France, and through three robust defensive layers to access Kalemegdan's inner core: first the Karadjordje Gate (dating to 1750), next the Inner Stambol Gate, and finally the Sahat Gate, beneath the clock tower. Divided internally into 'upper town' and 'lower town' areas, the fortress

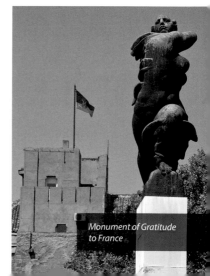

Monument of Gratitude to France

complex houses several sites of historic interest, including the *Victor* statue, the Ministry of Defence-run Military Museum and the Ružica Church. Helpful signs in English are dotted throughout.

On entering the inner walls of the fortress, bear left on the footpath to see one of the few remaining Ottoman buildings in Belgrade, the hexagonal **turbe of Damat Ali Pasha**, a mausoleum dating back to 1724 and recently refurbished with support from the Turkish government. Further on, you cannot miss Ivan Meštrović's statue of **The Victor ❸** (*Pobednik*), a 14m- (46ft-) high statue erected in 1928. Originally commissioned to mark Serbian victories in the First and Second Balkan Wars, work on *The Victor* was overtaken by events with the outbreak of World War I; in the end, it was instead dedicated to the tenth anniversary of the Serbian-Allied break-through on the Salonika Front. It also has a more general resonance

Damad Ali Pasha's mausoleum

as a symbol of Serbian military victories through the ages.

The Victor was originally intended to go up in Terazije, in the centre of town, but there was a hitch: the finished product was, as Rebecca West put it in *Black Lamb and Grey Falcon* in 1942, "recognizably male, so the municipality of Belgrade refused to set it up in the streets of the town, on the ground that it would offend female modesty". Positioned here instead ("buttocks to the fore," as West remarked),

Meštrović's *The Victor*

it directs the eye to the most splendid of Belgrade panoramas, where the majestic Danube meets its tributary, the Sava, and 'New Belgrade' beyond, on the opposite bank.

Looking across to the New Belgrade side, on a clear day you can pick out (from left to right) the Museum of Contemporary Art, the Genex Tower and the famous *blokovi*. In the foreground is the thickly wooded and uninhabited **Great War Island** (Veliko ratno ostrvo), so-named because of its strategic usefulness to various aggressors when bombarding Belgrade, and today noted for its rich birdlife.

RUŽICA CHURCH

To reach the sweetly named 'little rose church', or **Ružica Church** ❹ (Crkva Ružica), head down the stone steps to the lower level of the fortress. This gem-like, ivy-covered building, officially dedicated to the Most Holy Mother of God, was first built as an ammunition

Ružica Church

store, going on to become the garrison chapel when the Serbian army occupied Kalemegdan following the 1867 Ottoman handover. Symbolically, Turkish cannons were melted down to forge its bells.

The interior is a perfect microcosm of the Serbian Orthodox style, with its frescoes showing Serbia's medieval rulers holding the great monasteries they commissioned, and you can't miss the extraordinary chandelier adorned with hundreds of hanging bullet cases, dating from World War I.

Destroyed during World War I, the little rose church was rebuilt in 1925; the designer was Nikolai Krasnov, the White Russian emigré who helped create the Karadjordjević's exquisite Royal Palace at Dedinje (see page 73), and the same 'romantic nationalist' style is in evidence: note the idealized bronze figures on either side of the entrance, a medieval Serbian knight and a World War I infantryman.

MILITARY MUSEUM

The **Military Museum** ➎ (Vojni musej; Kalemegdan 66; tel: 011-334 3441, www.muzej.mod.gov.rs; Tues–Sun 10am–5pm, last entry at 4pm) is located on the highest level of the fortress complex; turn left to climb the stone steps immediately after the Inner Stambol Gate. Founded in 1878 to celebrate Serbian independence and today run by the Ministry of Defence, the museum is flanked by military hardware of both historic and conspicuously recent vintage. Inside, it offers both a useful chronological narrative of a national history thick with conflict, and an insight into the continuing struggle to assimilate and accept aspects of Serbia's recent past.

On the ground floor, the Military Museum's excellent collection showcases armaments and military garb used across the Balkans in the medieval and early modern eras, intercut with context on the kingdoms and conflicts of the period. Due prominence is given to the Battle of Kosovo of 1389 (see box, page 42). Moving on to the nineteenth and twentieth centuries, the uniforms on display track the evolution of a more European sensibility among Serbia's elite. Among the early twentieth-century exhibits, don't miss the text of

Missile launcher at the Military Museum

the declaration of war sent to the Kingdom of Serbia by the Austro-Hungarian Empire on 28 July 1914 (in French), and on the first floor, the bloodstained uniform worn by King Alexander Karadjordjević I when he was assassinated in Marseille in 1934. While English-language explanations are provided only sporadically, a trot through these galleries is a great way to get up to speed with Serbian history.

The museum's final gallery on the Yugoslav conflicts of the 1990s, however, strikes a dissonant note. Visitors are presented with information on Yugoslav and Serbian participation in UN peacekeeping missions, chiefly in Africa, but no mention is made of the UN peacekeepers deployed to Bosnia and Kosovo.

SERBIA AND KOSOVO

After the Battle of Kosovo Polje on 28 June 1389, fantasies of 'avenging Kosovo' were kept alive through epic oral poetry for centuries under Ottoman rule. The 'Kosovo myth' was hugely powerful in shaping national identity. The slogan *'Kosovo je Srbija'* (Kosovo is Serbia), visible graffitied around Belgrade, conveys both the idea that Kosovo is an indivisible part of Serbia, and that Serbian national identity began in Kosovo. Treasured medieval monasteries Dećani, Peć and Gračanica are on Kosovan soil; nationalist politicians have called Kosovo 'Serbia's Jerusalem'. It was thus Kosovo that Slobodan Milošević invoked to stoke Serbian nationalism as the end of Yugoslavia approached. In a 1988 speech, he said: "Every nation has one love that warms its heart. For Serbia it is Kosovo." The following year, on the 600th anniversary of the Battle of Kosovo Polje, he made his infamous Gazimestan speech on the 1389 battle site, presaging 'armed battles' in the future of Yugoslavia. *De facto* Serbian control of Kosovo ended in 1999, when NATO drove out Serbian forces. Kosovo declared independence in 2008.

On display are weapons captured from (in the words of the appended signs) 'Albanian terrorists', 'Croatian fascists', and the three American soldiers captured in 1999, but no narrative or context are offered around the break-up of the former Yugoslavia or the role of the JNA, Bosnian Serb Army and Serbian paramilitaries. In this little room, the challenges of regional reconciliation feel very real.

White lion at the zoo

ZOO

Just outside the Fortress walls, but within the Kalemegdan compound, is **Belgrade Zoo ⑥** (Mali Kalemegdan 8; tel: 011-262 4526, www.beozoovrt.rs; daily 9am–7pm), best reached by exiting the fortress from the Leopold Gate. Popular with local families, on display are a wide selection of animals, including rare white lions, an elephant, camels, kangaroos and meerkats. With its cramped and pungent set of enclosures, animal-lovers may not find this zoo a particularly uplifting example of the genre.

KNEZ MIHAILOVA AND STUDENTSKI TRG (STUDENTS' SQUARE)

From Kalemegdan, a web of streets stretches out to the south and east in a neat grid pattern, forming the historic core of Belgrade's

Knez Mihailova, the Old Town's main thoroughfare

enchanting Old Town. Bustling **Knez Mihailova** ❼ (as Kneza Mihaila is universally known) is the principal pedestrianized spine of the old town, running southeast from Kalemegdan along the ridge of the city.

Laid out in 1872 as part of the modernizing and unifying vision of city planner Emilijan Josimović, who aimed to bring Belgrade up to scratch as the cosmopolitan capital city of a new European nation, Knez Mihailova was named after prince (*knez*) Mihailo, Serbia's former Obrenović ruler, assassinated four years earlier in 1868. Thronging with shoppers by day, it is perhaps at its most charming as the evening draws in and Belgraders young and old begin their ritual evening walk.

The old town's prettiest facades are concentrated at the Kalemegdan end; it becomes progressively more commercialized as it approaches Trg Republike, where it transforms into busy, traffic-laden Terazije.

Turning left off Knez Mihailova about halfway down towards Trg Republike, you reach **Studentski Trg** ❽ (Students' Square), the intellectual and cultural heart of the city and home to one of Belgrade University's two campuses. Known as Royal Square from 1896 until 1946, the new Communist authorities rang in the changes, changing the name and converting the modernist 1934 Stock Exchange building at no.13 into the Ethnographic Museum, which it remains today. The impressive 1922 Faculty of Philology at no.3 and its neighbour, the 1932 Kolarac concert hall at no.5, overlook Academski Park (Academic Park) in the centre of the square. A major redevelopment of the square planned for the future to pedestrianize Studentski Trg, add a double-storey underground car park, and erect a memorial to former Prime Minister Zoran Djindjić – assassinated in 2003 (see page 83) – has been scaled back amid rumblings from many vocal critics.

ONLY UNITY SAVES THE SERBS

Looking at the Serbian flag, you may notice the 'four Cs' that surround the central cross. Though they originally symbolized firesteels, these 'four Cs' came by the time of the First Serbian Uprising (1804–13) to be interpreted as a nationalist slogan: *'samo sloga Srbina spasava'* ('only unity saves the Serbs' – the Cyrillic sound 's' transcribed with the Latin 'c'). The implication was that, with divided leadership, Serbs could never forge their national path. The phrase had resonance during the wars of the 1990s too, when Milošević advocated 'all Serbs in one state'. The phrase was adopted in nationalist graffiti, and during the Bosnian War of 1992–95, the fours Cs symbol was frequently found graffitied by Serbian fighters on the walls of houses previously occupied by ethnic Croats and Bosnian Muslims. You can still see it graffitied around Belgrade, too.

Kralja Petra ulica architecture

ETHNOGRAPHIC MUSEUM

The **Ethnographic Museum** ❾ (Etnografski Muzej, Studentski Trg 13; Tues–Fri 10am–5pm, Sun 9am–2pm) documents the social history of the pre-Yugoslav and Yugoslav periods through its collections of folk costumes and the paraphernalia of daily life. It offers a fascinating insight into the varied lives and customs of ordinary men and women from right across the diverse terrain of the former Yugoslavia, and is a valuable counterweight to the 'great men of history' feel to some of Belgrade's other major museums. The enlarged black-and-white photographs on display immortalize some truly outstanding moustaches, too.

Notable exhibits to look out for include a striking bridal cap from Raška (historic heartland of the early Serbian empire), with a kind of canopy projecting over the face, hung with bells, coins and brushes. Halfway up the stairs to the first-floor exhibition of period interiors and furnishings, keep your eyes peeled for the mounted *kilim* rug bearing the double-headed eagle and the logo CCCC (see box, page 45) – a neat blend of Ottoman form and Serbian patriotic function.

CATHEDRAL AND SURROUNDS

Kralja Petra ulica slices through Knez Mihailova not far from the Kalemegdan end. Turn right onto it, heading downhill towards the river, to find **St Michael's Cathedral ⑩** (daily 7am–9pm; free) on the corner with Kneza Sime Markovica 3. The Cathedral was commissioned by Knez (prince) Miloš Obrenović as a celebration of Serbia's new found freedom following the 1830 grant of autonomy from the Sultan (see page 20). Built in the Baroque style in 1840, St Michael's was deliberately more Europeanized than the Serbian tradition of church design dictated, with tall

The Residence of Princess Ljubica

Cobbled Kosančićev venac

spires instead of the squat Byzantine-style cupolas that crown Belgrade's other major churches, St Mark's and St Sava's.

St Michael's became the site of royal coronations, weddings and funerals and is technically still Belgrade's only cathedral – although St Sava's in Vračar is often referred to as such. The Obrenović dynasty's family tombs are here, as well as part of the relics of Tsar Lazar, brought here to provide symbolic legitimacy for the Obrenović dynasty. Lazar – the Serbian prince whose troops were defeated at the 1389 Battle of Kosovo – was an important figure in Serbia's medieval mythology: in the epic poems he was said to have chosen the heavenly kingdom over his earthly one.

Immediately opposite the Cathedral is the **Serbian Orthodox Church Museum ⑪** (entrance from Kneza Sime Markovica 3; Mon–Fri 9am–4pm), housed in a beautiful Serbian Patriarchate building designed by Russian émigré architect Viktor Lukomski in 1935, incorporating Serbian national motifs such as the double-headed eagle in its Art Deco style. The collection includes heavily jewelled Bibles, crucifixes, icons, ornate vestments and other ecclesiastical paraphernalia.

Just around the corner at Kneza Sime Markovica 8 stands the sugar-white **Residence of Princess Ljubica ⑫** (Konak Kneginje Ljubice; www.mgb.org.rs; Tues–Thurs & Sat 10am–5pm, Fri 10am until 6pm, Sun until 2pm). This Balkan-style residence, built in 1829 by Prince Miloš Obrenović for his wife, Princess Ljubica, gives a lively flavour of the transformation of tastes as Serbia gradually emerged from under Ottoman rule to join the European community of nations.

As part of restoration work on the mansion, the clutch of rooms has been designed so that, if you visit them clockwise, they illustrate Serbia's journey from Ottoman influence in the early nineteenth century (look out for the low-slung banks of seating and on-site hammam) to speedy and self-aware Europeanization by the late 1900s.

Don't miss the evocative portrait of Prince (Knez) Miloš himself, resplendent in a large red hat and golden epaulettes, posing in front of one of Belgrade's largest mosques of the period.

Busy Trg Republike

BELGRADE'S 'MONTMARTRE'

Veering off Kneza Sime Markovica, one street further down is Kosančićev venac, a sloping, cobbled street which offers beautiful views across the Sava River, particularly by night, with the bridges atmospherically lit up. The three crescents in this part of town – **Kosančićev venac**, **Topličin venac** and **Obilićev venac** – were built as part of Belgrade's late nineteenth-century beautification programme and are named after three Serbian medieval heroes who died defending their country in the 1389 Battle of Kosovo. 'Sworn brothers' commemorated in Serbian oral poetry, they were Milan Toplica, Ivan Kosančić and – the most famous in Serbian folk memory – Miloš Obilić, who entered Sultan Murat's tent and stabbed him to death.

The three crescents have had a (somewhat aspirational) rebrand as 'Belgrade's Montmartre', with soft street-lighting installed. Although it's not a comparison to be taken too seriously, this is certainly a charming corner of the city for kicking back with drinks or cocktails. Pedestrianized Topličin venac is particularly pretty festooned with fairy lights of an evening.

In Proleće Park, just off Topličin venac, you can't miss the **Vojvoda Vuk statue** ⓭ (literally,

National Museum

'war-leader wolf'), full of dynamism and ruthlessness. The 1936 statue honours Vojin Popović, who earned his nickname as a commander of the *četniks* (independence fighters) during the First and Second Balkan Wars. Cut short in his prime, he died in 1916 on the Salonika Front.

TRG REPUBLIKE (REPUBLIC SQUARE)

> ### See you at the Crossroads
>
> The name 'Dorćol' comes from the Turkish words for four (*dört*) and road (*yol*); so-named because, in higgledy-piggledy Ottoman-era Belgrade, the clear delineation of four roads at the crossroad where Kralja Petra met Cara Dušana was unusual enough to be worth remarking on.

At the southeastern end of Knez Mihailova lies the city's main square, **Trg Republike** ⑭ (Republic Square). In Ottoman times, this was the outer limit of Belgrade, marked by a major defensive gate (the Stambol Gate). Remodelled in the 1860s, Trg Republike's most picturesque aspect today is gained facing the National Museum, with the National Theatre to your right.

The bronze equestrian **Prince (*Knez*) Mihailo statue** ⑮ atop his horse dates to 1882. It is a popular meeting spot for modern Belgraders, who will agree to meet '*kod konja*' (by the horse). Son of Miloš Obrenović, Mihailo ruled Serbia from 1839 until 1842 and again from 1860 onward, until his assassination in 1868 in Koštunjak Forest, the royal hunting ground just outside Belgrade.

Mihailo's horse points in the direction of the historic heartlands to the south, including Kosovo and Raška, that were known as 'Old Serbia' and which Serbian nationalists still dreamed of liberating. Serbia would regain this territory only half a century later, in the Second Balkan War. On the granite pedestal beneath his statue

Bajrakli Mosque at prayer time

are the names of the six fortified cities that were the last Ottoman strongholds until Serbia finally gained full *de facto* independence in 1867, in the penultimate year of his reign: Šabac, Smederevo, Kladovo, Užice and Soko Grad.

NATIONAL MUSEUM

The **National Museum** 16 (Narodni muzej, 1a Republic Square; www.narodnimuzej.rs; Tues, Weds, Fri & Sun 10am–6pm, Thurs & Sat noon–8pm) is both a national museum and a national gallery; the majority of the more modern exhibits are artworks. Built in 1901 as a bank, the Communists commandeered the building to house the collection of the National Museum, itself established in 1844 in support of the development of a Serbian national consciousness. Following a fifteen-year renovation completed in 2018, the art and artefacts are well presented, with good lighting and clear English-language signage.

The first-floor galleries focus on the medieval heritage of Serbia, including the finely crafted (and well-preserved) jewellery of the medieval Serbian kings and princes. Moving on to the art of the emerging nation in the eighteenth to nineteenth centuries, look out in particular for Jovan Isajlović the Younger's memorable composition, *Death of Prince Milan* (1839), which offers a glimpse of Serbian fashion and culture in its early years as a semi-autonomous principality. Another notable work is Stevan Aleksić's powerful *Burning of the Remains of Saint Sava* (1912): painted at the height of the Balkan Wars, this was art as a call to arms.

The top-floor galleries focus on Yugoslav art of the twentieth century, beginning with Serbia's own Impressionists and moving on to post-war Yugoslav art. The stylistic shift to socialist realism is marked by Boža Ilić's monumental artwork, *Testing the Terrain in New Belgrade* (1948), which depicts the volunteer work parties who built the new city on the Sava's west bank in a surge of hope for a brighter future.

DORĆOL

The dense lattice of streets sloping downhill from behind the National Museum is **Dorćol**, known in the late Ottoman era as the Turkish town or *Turska varoš*, reflecting its ethnic concentration. The area was described by Roman

Jewish Historical Museum

The 20/44 bar in Skadarlija

Zmorski, a Polish writer visiting in the mid-nineteenth century, as "a wonderful view of the East thrown within a hand's reach of Europe". Dorćol was smartened up significantly in the 1860s and 1870s, with town planners imposing a neat grid system of narrow streets rising to the ridge of Knez Mihailova, and down towards Cara Dušana.

Today, it retains that orderly layout, upmarket bistros and boutiques mixing with graffitied blocks and dishevelled fin-de-siècle buildings in its narrow, interlocking streets. Dorćol is both well-heeled and hipsterish, and the visitor in search of a good spot for coffee, craft beer or cocktails is spoilt for choice here.

Heading downhill along Kralja Petra from Knez Mihailova, turn left onto Gospodar Jevremova street to find **Bajrakli Mosque** ⑰ located at no.11: the only remaining mosque of more than 200 that studded Belgrade's skyline in the Ottoman era. The building dates back to 1575 and is named the Bajrakli-džamija after the 'barjak', a flag flown from its minaret to signal the start of prayers to surrounding mosques.

In 2004, the mosque was set ablaze in retaliation for anti-Serb riots in Kosovo which targeted a number of churches – a bleak continuation of the Western Balkan tradition of targeting religious heritage. Muslims today make up some three percent of Serbia's population (excluding Kosovo), and the mosque's survival as an active place of worship is an important reminder of Belgrade's more multi-ethnic past.

Returning to Kralja Petra, at no.71 you'll find the **Jewish Historical Museum** ⓲ (Jevrejski istorijski muzej; Kralja Petra 71; www.jimbeograd.org; Mon–Fri 10am–2pm). In the Ottoman era, Dorćol included the Jewish quarter. With the decimation of the Jewish population during the war, Serbia was the first Nazi-occupied territory in Europe to be declared *Judenrein*, or 'free of Jews' (see page 80).

This small but important museum, located on the second floor of Belgrade's Jewish Community Centre, presents a collection of maps, photographs and artefacts such as Torah scrolls documenting the history of the Jewish community in the Balkans. Many of the documents and photographs here were gathered in the late

National Parliament

Palatial Plenty

Belgrade boasts five palaces built by Serbia's two rival royal houses. A nineteenth-century French visitor expansively (or ironically) described Miloš Obrenović's *konak* at Topčider as 'the Versailles of the Serbian Princes'. In the 1860s, the 'Old Palace' and 'New Palace' were added, and finally in the interwar years, the two royal palaces at Dedinje.

1940s to bear witness to the crimes perpetrated by the Nazi and Ustaša regimes during World War II.

One street along at Cara Uroša 20 is the **Gallery of Frescoes ⓳** (Galerija fresaka; www.narodnimuzej.rs; Tues, Wed & Fri 10am–5pm, Thurs & Sat noon–8pm, Sun 10am–2pm). Closed for renovation at the time of writing, the gallery contains replicas of over 1,000 precious medieval frescoes dating from the eleventh to fifteenth centuries, medieval Serbia's golden age. The originals are scattered across the great monasteries, several of them in Kosovo; their luscious pastels, vivid use of pattern and gold accenting are faithfully reproduced here.

SKADARLIJA

East of Dorćol, just beyond Francuska, is **Skadarlija ⓴**, Belgrade's former bohemian quarter. Once the haunt of artists and writers, Skadarlija – which is really no more than a single street, Skadarska ulica – is today firmly dedicated to dining, drinking and music. By day it feels rather disconsolate, rose petals from the night before trodden into the uneven cobbles, but by night Skadarska comes alive, lusty singing and heart-rending folk ballads erupting from the restaurants' dining rooms and terraces. Clichéd it may be, but a night out in Skadarlija accompanied by a traditional tambura orchestra is an essential Belgrade experience.

BETWEEN THE BOULEVARDS: WIDER CITY CENTRE

Beyond the Old Town, a cluster of attractions lies sandwiched between two busy boulevards, Bulevar Kralja Aleksandra (once the Roman Via Militaris) and Bulevar Despota Stefana: namely, the Parliament Building (Skupština Srbije), Tašmajdan Park and St Mark's Church, and just off busy Takovska street, the Botanical Gardens.

Heading away from the Old Town, Terazije slices through the commercial and business heart of the city. Pause a moment to admire the **Hotel Moskva**, a Belgrade landmark built in 1908 in the Secessionist style, its tiled facades giving it a distinctive sheen. In 1926, Lena Jovičić, a Scottish-Serbian writer, thought it looked so incongruous among the squat surrounding buildings that it

Statue of Tsar Nicholas II

"seemed like a pelican in the wilderness". In front of the hotel is the 1860 Miloš Obrenović fountain (also known as the Terazijska česma, the Terazije drinking fountain).

NATIONAL PARLIAMENT

Past Nikola Pašić Square and its splashing fountain, you reach the **Parliament Building ㉑**, home to Serbia's National Assembly and its 250 MPs (Skupština Srbije, Nikola Pašić Square; www.parlament. rs). The location was chosen for symbolic reasons: Belgrade's main mosque, the Batal džamija, stood here in Ottoman times. The Parliament's foundation stone was laid in 1907, but the building was not ready for use until 1936. Nikolai Krasnov, a White Russian émigré who also designed the interiors for the Royal Palace at Dedinje, was the architect. The two statues at the front, named

St Mark's Church

'black horses at play', were added in 1938.

This building is no stranger to political dramas: it continued to serve as the House of Representatives throughout the post-war Communist era, and in October 2000, flags waved from its burning windows as demonstrators stormed the building, forcing President Slobodan Milošević to finally concede the success of his opponent, Vojislav Koštunica, at the ballot-box. Individual visits to the Parliament Building can be booked in advance via the Tourist Office of Belgrade (first Sat of each month; tel: 011-263 5622).

Tašmajdan Park

Straight opposite the Parliament stands Pionirski Park, its neat flowerbeds bordered on either side by two notable pieces of civic architecture: the Belgrade city assembly (Beogradski skupština), which occupies the Old Palace (Stari Dvor) built for the Obrenović dynasty in 1884, and the rather greyed, sad-looking Presidential palace (Predsednički Dvor), built in 1911–22 as the 'New Palace', this time for the Karadjordjević royal family. Like the National Parliament, these two look their finest illuminated at night.

Directly across the road that runs behind the park – Kralja Milana – you'll find the eye-catching **statue of Tsar Nicholas II**, Russia's last tsar. In the ornate Russian imperial style, it is in fact a modern piece, donated to the city in 2014 to celebrate Russian-Serbian friendship.

Honouring the victims of the NATO bombing of the Chinese Embassy

On a side street near the National Parliament, the surprisingly absorbing **Automobile Museum** ㉒ (Automuseum, Majke Jevrosime 30; www.automuseumbgd.com; daily 9.30am–8pm) traces the rapid evolution of car design over the twentieth century, from early models such as the 1908 Citroën through the glamour years (featuring Tito's Cadillac) to utilitarian little 1960s and 1970s family cars. The display of colourized images from the September 1939 Belgrade Grand Prix, held on the day Britain and France declared war on Nazi Germany, makes a fascinating contrast with today's Belgrade.

ST MARK'S AND TAŠMAJDAN

A couple of hundred metres further along Bulevar Kralja Aleksandra from the Parliament Building, at the north end of Tašmajdan Park, rises **St Mark's Church** ㉓ (Crkva Svetog Marka, Bulevar Kralja Aleksandra 17; daily 8am–7pm; free). Modelled on the beautiful Gračanica monastery near Pristina in Kosovo, St Mark's was built in 1932–39 to mark the spot where, in 1830, ceremonial tents were pitched and the *hatti-sherif* (decree of the Sultan) was read to Knez Miloš by Ottoman dignitaries in front of the assembled crowds. Independence would wait another 37 years, but this was a milestone moment, making Miloš hereditary prince (or *knez*) of Serbia, now a semi-autonomous principality within the Ottoman Empire.

The interior of St Mark's is plain and austere – unfinished, in fact, as decoration work was interrupted by the outbreak of World War II. Against the blank walls, the few elements of ornamentation stand out in stark contrast: the curved golden mosaic of the Virgin and Child behind the iconostasis; the tomb of the revered medieval emperor Stefan Dušan (1308–55), flanked by two soldiers and a prodigious candelabra. Near the door is the tomb of Patriarch German, who from 1958–90 played a key role in protecting the Serbian Orthodox church's position in the Communist state. St Mark's **crypt** (closed to visitors) also contains the bodies of the unfortunate last

NATO BOMBING OF BELGRADE

In the spring of 1999, NATO launched US-led air strikes to force Yugoslav President Slobodan Milošević to withdraw his troops from Kosovo. NATO countries expected the bombing to last a few days before Milošević capitulated; it went on for 78 days. According to the independent international NGO Human Rights Watch, it resulted in around 500 civilian casualties, sped up the process of the displacement of ethnic Albanians from their homes and, in the latter stages, included targeting sites of dubious military value such as the Radio Television of Serbia (RTS) building. NATO strikes also accidentally hit the Chinese Embassy, killing three Chinese journalists and injuring several Embassy workers; a major diplomatic incident that China's Ambassador to the UN described as a 'crime against humanity'. While Milošević and his Kosovo campaign were far from universally popular in Serbia, citizens defiantly came together in the face of NATO bombardment, particularly in the early days, holding rallies and open-air concerts. The experience of being bombed by NATO still plays into ambivalent views of the West and divisions over Serbia's future geopolitical orientation.

Nikola Tesla Museum

Obrenović king, King Alexander I, and Queen Draga, assassinated in 1903 (see page 20).

Immediately behind the church, **Tašmajdan Park** ㉔ was built on the site of a former stone quarry (hence the name: 'taš' from Turkish, meaning stone and 'majdan', quarry). In the First Serbian Uprising, Karadjordje's insurgents hid in the resulting subterranean tunnels to spring surprise attacks on the Ottomans.

The park contains two small but hard-hitting **plaques commemorating the NATO bombing** of Belgrade, which took place in spring 1999. The first, located along a footpath (to the left, with St Mark's Church just behind you), is a roughly hewn stone printed with the stark question, *Зашто?* (Why?). It lists the 16 journalists killed in the air strike which hit the Radio-Television Serbia (RTS) building. Today, the gutted wreck of the RTS building can clearly be seen just beyond the edge of the park, behind the stone. The second memorial plaque is a heart-shaped monument at the centre of the park depicting a little girl holding a teddy bear; it commemorates the children killed during the NATO campaign. You will naturally wish to be discreet when in the vicinity of the plaques.

For a welcome touch of tranquillity in the city centre, head north along trafficky Takovska from the Parliament Building to reach the **Jevremovac Botanical Gardens ㉕** (Jevremovac Botaničke Bašte, Takovska 43; www.jevremovac.bio.bg.ac.rs; May–Oct daily 9am–5pm). These compact but well-maintained gardens, first opened

SCARS ON THE CITY

A short walk from the centre of the Vračar district are the ruins of the **Ministry of Defence** and the **Ministry of the Interior**, both seriously damaged in the 1999 NATO bombings and left untouched for over twenty years. There is periodic talk of building something in their place, but for now they remain, visceral and unforgettable scars on the face of the city. Although these sites are now an established stopping-off point in some Belgrade tours, it is wise to be discreet and avoid taking photographs or looking too conspicuously.

To find these sites, walk one block south of the Beogradjanka building, via Manjež park, and head downhill along Nemanjina – which remains the heart of the government quarter (the Ministries of Justice and European Integration have their headquarters here). At the intersection with Kneza Miloša, the two sites are unmissable on opposite sides of the street; the Defence Ministry (Ministarstvo Odbrane) is on the right, a shell of what was a vast corner block. Nearby banners inveigh against the breakaway territory of Kosovo ('Albanian terrorists') being allowed to join Interpol. The anger remains strongly felt: Serbian President Alexander Vučić has said of the 1999 bombing, "Their goal was clear: to beat us and humiliate us, and then give part of our territory to someone else."

Neo-Byzantine Church of St Sava

in 1874 as part of the project of 'Europeanizing' Belgrade, are a delightful place to take a peaceful break from the relentless thrum of the city.

The centrepiece is the original 1892 greenhouse, renovated with EU funding and containing species such as banana trees, aloe vera and the hedgehog agave; the gardens as a whole feature some 2,000 species of tree and herbaceous plant.

VRAČAR

South of the Bulevar Kralja Aleksandra, the Vračar district is a 20- to 30-minute walk from the city centre, straight along Terazije and Kralja Milana. As you descend Kralja Milana, look out for the building affectionately called by locals the **Beogradjanka** ('Belgrade Lady') – officially, the *Palata Beograd* (Palace of Belgrade) which was, when built in 1974, Belgrade's tallest skyscraper at 101m

(331ft) tall. Rivalling Dorćol as a hub of Belgrade's café culture, Vračar's visual focal point is the monumental Church of St Sava, set on the plateau beyond Trg Slavija. The excellent Nikola Tesla Museum on leafy Krunska street is the other highlight here.

Turning off Kralja Milana onto pedestrianized Njegoševa, lined with tempting cafés such as *Bacio gelato* (see page 92), it's a 10-minute walk to the flower-strewn, nineteenth-century townhouse that is home to the fascinating **Nikola Tesla Museum** ㉖ (Krunska 51; www.tesla-museum.org; Mon–Fri 10am–5pm, Sat & Sun 10am–6pm). A tireless inventor with exceptional vision and imagination, Tesla died with hundreds of patents to his name in 27 countries, in addition to his ground-breaking work on alternating current (AC).

His 'big idea' – AC– apparently sprang into his mind while walking in a park in Budapest with a friend, reciting verses from Goethe's *Faust*. English-speaking guides give excellent interactive demonstrations of a few of Tesla's many inventions (be warned, brave volunteers will receive small electric shocks on their hands). Guided tours run throughout the day.

The gilded crypt inside St Sava

ST SAVA'S CHURCH

Deeper into Vračar, continuing along Kralja Milana away from the city centre, you can't miss the imposing

St Sava's Church ㉗ ahead of you (Hram svetog Save, Svetosavski Trg; www.hramsvetogsave.com; daily 7am–8pm). This vast neo-Byzantine structure peers down upon the city from the Vračar plateau, topped by a four-tonne gold cross and encircled by a large open piazza. Sometimes called a temple (in deference to its proportions) or even a cathedral, it is strictly speaking just a plain old church (St Michael's in the Old Town is the seat of the Belgrade bishop, or *metropolitan*).

The youngest son of the famed medieval king Stefan Nemanja, St Sava's key achievement was to secure *autocephaly* (independence) for the church from the Byzantine Patriarch in Constantinople in 1219, thus founding the Serbian Orthodox Church. His enduring legacy was thus to make Orthodoxy a key

BETWEEN RUSSIA AND EUROPE

Serbia's political ties with Russia rest on centuries-old notions of Orthodox and Slavic kinship. When Serbia was at its most isolated under Milošević, Russia was its key backer on the global stage, and Russia has continued to use its international influence to staunchly oppose Kosovo's independence. In 2014, Serbia began its accession negotiations with the European Union (EU). In the same year it also entered a strategic partnership with Russia, and in 2019 it signed a free trade deal with the Eurasian Economic Union (set up by Russia to rival the EU). Serbia has refused to follow the EU's sanctions regime on Russia, as is expected of would-be member states, and has received a number of Russian donations of military equipment such as fighter jets and tanks, which it displays in military parades. On the 'soft power' side, Russia continues to bolster its reputation in Serbia through projects such as the refurbishment of St Sava's dome.

Brankov bridge connects the Old Town and New Belgrade

aspect of Serbian identity; for centuries under Ottoman occupation, the church was a conduit for proto-national sentiment. Sava was canonized on his death in 1236, but in 1594 the Ottoman authorities – aiming to suppress a rebellion ongoing at the time – exhumed his remains and burned them on Vračar plateau. Unsurprisingly, this had the opposite effect, inflaming Serbian national sentiment: see Stevan Aleksić's powerful painting of the event in the National Museum (see page 52).

In newly independent Serbia, there was enthusiasm for a commemorative church at the spot where Sava's remains had been burned. Building work began in 1935, but was interrupted by World War II. After a pause, it recommenced in 1984, and today specialist decorative (largely mosaic) work on the cavernous interior continues, part of a joint project with the Russian Culture Ministry and part-funded by Russian energy company Gazprom-Neft. Although the delicate and painstaking restoration work is

SALA 2
**Fond memorijalnog centra
Josip Broz Tito**
*Vladarski prostor, lični predmeti
i simboli vlasti*

HALL 2
**Memorial Centre
Josip Broz Tito Fund**
*Sovereign's space, personal objects
and symbols of power*

*Tito memorabilia at the Museum
of Yugoslavia*

expected to continue for several more years, St Sava's remains well worth visiting, both for its monumental exteriors and for its completed **crypt**, glowing with gold, where key figures from Serbian history (Despot Stefan, Tsar Lazar et al) parade across the walls and ceiling. All have 'Sv' (for *sveti* – saint) in front of their names, underlining the way in which the medieval Serbian kingdoms threaded together temporal and spiritual power.

In front of the church, facing down towards Bulevar Oslobodjenja, the **statue of Karadjordje** lowers darkly over the city, curved sword in hand (see page 19). This striking 1979 statue certainly conveys something of the man who Rebecca West, travelling the Balkans 100 years after his death, described as a "moody and valiant giant, who was no mere springing tiger but possessed real military genius … tall even for a race of tall men, with burning eyes, wild coal-black hair, a face that was still handsome though deeply scarred".

SAVAMALA

South of Brankov bridge, which leads to New Belgrade on the west bank of the Sava River, is Savamala, meaning 'the Sava quarter' – one of Belgrade's most run-down neighbourhoods. This former industrial area epitomizes shabby-chic: eerily empty by day, by night it plays host to some of Belgrade's coolest alternative clubs, such as Mladost/Ludost and KC Grad. Savamala is also home to the multi-million 'Belgrade Waterfront' development – thousands of luxury apartments huddled along the Sava waterfront, along with a clutch of shops, restaurants and bars. The waterfront

TITO: THE MAN WHO MADE YUGOSLAVIA

Born in rural Croatia in 1892, Josip Broz (nicknamed Tito) spent part of World War I in a Russian labour camp in the Urals, subsequently joining the Red Army. In 1937 he became secretary general of the Yugoslav Communist Party. During the war, he led the Partisans, the Communist guerrilla army. In 1945, the Partisans liberated Belgrade and Tito founded the Socialist Federal Republic of Yugoslavia. Yugoslavia broke with Moscow in 1948 and, instead of joining the Warsaw Pact, Tito carved out a distinct geopolitical role for Yugoslavia, co-founding the Non-Aligned Movement, the grouping of 'global South' countries seeking independence from the Cold War's twin superpowers, in 1961. His brand of Communism also rejected state ownership in favour of 'workers' self-management'. The citizens of Yugoslavia enjoyed stability, relative prosperity, and the chance to travel visa-free to more countries than people from any other country in the world, thanks to good relations with both East and West. High levels of popular support for Tito and his regime endured for four decades, and the cult of personality persisted even after his death.

Sava Promenada has become a popular attraction here, and a much-anticipated landmark skyscraper – the 168m- (551ft-) high Belgrade Tower – is scheduled for completion in 2022.

Although Savamala is close by Kosančićev venac, one of the prettiest parts of the Old Town, there is an abrupt change of tone under Brankov bridge, and most young Belgraders coming here at night get to their club or bar of choice using a pre-booked taxi (see page 132) or the Car.Go app.

DEDINJE

Spanning the hillside to the south of the city is Dedinje, the affluent neighbourhood once famous for its vineyards that is now the Embassy quarter. It is home to two of Belgrade's most engaging

Tito's tomb in the House of Flowers mausoleum

historical sights: the Museum of Yugoslavia and the Royal Palaces, residences of the last Yugoslav royals.

THE MUSEUM OF YUGOSLAVIA

Renovations at the excellent **Museum of Yugoslavia** ㉘ (Muzej jugoslavije, Mihaila Mike Jankovića 6; www.muzej-jugoslavije.org/en; Wed–Sun 10am–6pm) have not entirely removed the lingering sense that one is here to pay homage to the achievements of former Yugoslav President Tito (see box, page 69). These were, of course, considerable: he acted as a figurehead who Yugoslavs of all ethnicities could coalesce around, brought relative prosperity, and steered an almost impossibly delicate path between East and West during the Cold War years. As Churchill's wartime envoy, Fitzroy Maclean, wrote: "here at last was a Communist who did not need to refer everything to the 'competent authorities', to look up the Party line at every step. He himself was the competent authority and, as for the Party line, he knew it instinctively, or perhaps even evolved it as he went along."

Today, the nostalgia for Tito is alive and well: the museum complex still receives an upsurge of visitors on Tito's birthday (25 May) each year, and a 2016 Gallup poll found that Serbia was the ex-Yugoslav country where the highest proportion of people regretted the breakup of Yugoslavia. To reach the museum, take bus 40 or 41 from Tašmajdan Park.

A Yugoslav Inheritance

As the other states of the former Yugoslavia seceded, Serbia inherited many of the trappings of the former federation: not just its capital city, army, government buildings and palaces, but also the domain name .yu – which was only replaced by .rs in 2010, and is preserved as Museum of Yugoslavia's only 'digital exhibit'.

The first museum on the site, the **25 May Museum**, was built in 1962 to house the many birthday presents that Tito received from associations of workers, youth and schoolchildren across Yugoslavia. These were largely relay batons: a 'Relay of Youth' was run right across the diverse terrain of Yugoslavia on the 25 May every year from 1948 onward, marking the unity of this once-divided territory. Celebrated as a national holiday, the relays stopped only in 1988, eight years after Tito's death. On display today is a small selection of the 22,000 relay batons he was given, each topped with a miniature symbol of the group or association concerned: ears of corn, tanks, a box camera and a dinky little radiator.

In the **House of Flowers mausoleum** (Kuća Cveća), originally designed in 1975 as Tito's winter garden, is his white marble coffin, the name etched in simple gold lettering. Tropical flowers bloom

The Royal Compound

around it, and large windows afford splendid views over the former Yugoslav capital. Visitors can scroll through a digitized version of the book of condolences signed by ambassadors and foreign dignitaries at the time of Tito's death.

ROYAL COMPOUND

Not far from the Tito Museum is the **Royal Compound** 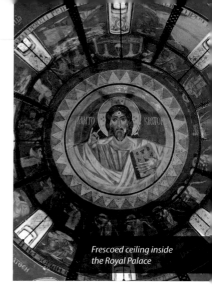 (Dvorski complex; Bulevar Kneza Aleksandra Karadjordjevića

Frescoed ceiling inside the Royal Palace

96; tel: 011-306 4000; www.royal.rs). Visits are permitted as part of a guided tour only; English-language tours lasting around 2.5 hours are organized by the Tourist Organization of Belgrade (TOB) on Knez Mihailova 5 (tel: 011-263 5622; bginfo.knezmihailova@tob.rs; www.tob.rs; Wed, Sat & Sun April–Nov). The palace compound was developed in the 1920s and 1930s by the Karadjordjević dynasty who ruled the Kingdom of Yugoslavia. There are two palaces here, set in extensive grounds: the more elaborate Royal Palace and the simpler White Palace. A visit offers a fascinating glimpse into the preoccupations and privileges of a deposed monarchy. In 1947, the properties of the former royal family were confiscated – along with their Yugoslav citizenship – and the Dedinje palaces were commandeered for Tito's personal use.

The descendants of Serbia's last royals moved back in 2001, and now split their time between Belgrade and London. Although the House of Karadjordjević has no constitutional status in Serbia, the state funds and protects the former royal family and the palaces, which were restored to them by the Serbian High Court in 2015. The luckiest visitors may get a quick greeting from a royal ('HRH Crown Prince Alexander' or 'Princess Katherine'); they reside on the upper floors. Crown Prince Alexander II is the son of Serbia's last monarch, King Peter II, who went into exile in 1941. Alexander was born at Claridge's Hotel in London in 1945; Queen Elizabeth II is his godmother. He served as a British Army officer and became British Army Ski Champion in 1972. Photography is not permitted inside, but the official royal photographer meets tours and will take a snap for a small fee.

The **Royal Palace** (Kraljevski dvor) was built at the behest of the ill-fated Alexander I in 1929. The exterior is clad in white marble from Brač Island in Croatia. The entrance hall is adorned with replica frescoes from the venerated monasteries at Dečani (in Kosovo) and Sopoćani. The Serbian chief architect was supported by Nikolai Krasnov and Victor Lukomsky, both White Russian émigrés, and the basement is a homage to their lost homeland, the vaulted ceiling depicting scenes from Rimsky-Korsakov's ballet *Scheherazade*. Also in the basement are Tito's private cinema (Westerns were reportedly his favourites), and the 'whisper room', with

White Palace interior

fountains designed to tinkle noisily enough to allow for the discreet exchange of political confidences. Ground-floor highlights include a self-portrait by Ivan Meštrović (sculptor of *The Victor* at Kalemegdan), and the Blue Room, which offers commanding views towards the old royal hunting ground at Koštunjak.

Zemun

The **White Palace** (Beli dvor) is a more modest affair – though still impressive. Building work was begun in 1934 by Alexander I, as a residence for his three sons, but he never saw it in its finished state. He was assassinated in Marseille in 1934 by a Macedonian assassin linked to the extreme Croat nationalist group, the Ustaša (see page 24). The assassination and its aftermath were captured on camera – one of the first pieces of live footage of a major political event, and still available on Pathé newsreel. After World War II, Tito resided in the White Palace, building a spa centre with outdoor pool (now abandoned). In the 1990s, Slobodan Milošević hosted international diplomats here; today the building is hired out for high society weddings and receptions.

TOPČIDER PARK

Also to the south of the city, but a 30-minute walk from the Museum of Yugoslavia, is the **Residence of Prince Miloš** ㉚ in Topčider Park (Konak Kneza Miloša, Topčiderski Park; 5km (3 miles) south of the city centre; tel: 011-266 0442; www.imus.org.rs/en/konak-kneza-milosa;

The mighty Danube

Europe's second-biggest river (after the Volga) cuts through ten countries, from the mountains of the Black Forest in Germany to the Black Sea in Ukraine. It runs for 588km (365 miles) through Serbia (where it is called the *Dunav* or Дунав) and through three other European capitals: Vienna, Bratislava and Budapest.

April–Sept Tues–Sun 10am–5pm, Oct–March until 4pm). Prince Miloš Obrenović built the residence (*konak*) on the edge of Topčider Park from 1832–34, a mark of his newly elevated status as hereditary ruler of the principality of Serbia. The *konak* is in the traditional Balkan style, an architectural echo of the residence of his wife, Princess Ljubica, in the Old Town. The Balkan-Oriental style period interiors are infused with the tastes of the early nineteenth-century elite, all low benches and luxuriant carpeting. The first floor houses an exhibition on the Second Serbian Uprising (which Milos Obrenović led). To get here from the city centre, take tram 3 from outside Tašmajdan park, and get off at the Topčiderski stop.

NEW BELGRADE AND ZEMUN

No trip to the city would be complete without venturing across the Sava to take in the post-war architecture and riverside charms of **New Belgrade** (Novi Beograd), strung along the west bank of the Sava and nudging south of the Danube. The paved waterfronts in New Belgrade and Zemun are the perfect place to take in the immensity of the Danube, measuring on average half a kilometre across, and to take the pace off city life.

New Belgrade also plays host to several stellar examples of Brutalist architecture, expressions of a faded post-war utopia. The *blokovi* or 'blocks', built with a proud emphasis on function over form, communal living over individual privilege, now enjoy a kind of cult status. Further north-west is **Zemun**, a settlement historically held by the Austro-Hungarians, famed for its awe-inspiring Danube views and excellent fish restaurants.

NEW BELGRADE

New Belgrade covers a wide – and chiefly residential – area, with the sights of chief interest concentrated in the northeastern tip, around the confluence of the Sava and the Danube (or *ušće*). Cross Brankov bridge (Brankov most) by bus or taxi to reach **Friendship Park ㉛** (Park Prijatelstva), crisscrossed with fresh, well-lit paths for walking, cycling and jogging. Global leaders from across the political spectrum, from Kim Il-Sung and Fidel Castro to Jimmy Carter, planted

Museum of Contemporary Art

trees here in Tito's lifetime as a sign of friendship with Yugoslavia. Look out too for the towering *Eternal Flame* monument, a memorial to the civilians killed in the 1999 NATO bombing: the brainchild of Slobodan Milošević's wife, Mirjana Marković, it was unveiled in June 2000, four months before her husband's fall from power.

On the river's edge nearby, and stretching right around the Danube and Sava waterfronts, are the famous *splavovi* or floating rafts, variously used as restaurants, hostels and clubs.

A ten-minute walk around the curve of the rivers is the 1965 **Museum of Contemporary Art** ㉜ (Muzej savremene umetnosti, Ušće 10, blok 15; www.msub.org.rs; Mon & Wed–Fri noon–8pm, Sat & Sun 10am–8pm), with its distinctive cubic design a fitting complement to the utopianism of the New Belgrade project. Overlooking the confluence of the rivers (or *ušće*), the museum is clearly visible across the Sava from Kalemegdan. Inside, the focus is on

---

BELGRADE'S BRUTALIST BEAUTIES

Most accessible from the *splavovi* on the Danube is the monumental 1959 H-shaped **Palace of Serbia** (Palata Srbije) or **SIV** (the former seat of the Yugoslav Federal Executive Council) on Bulevar Mihajla Pupina 2. The 1977 **Sava Centar** on Milentija Popovića, at blok 19, continues to fulfil its intended function as the beating cultural heart of New Belgrade, hosting concerts (see page 94). Further west, and deep into the blokovi at blok 1 is the 1977–80 **Genex Tower** or 'West Gate' on Narodnih heroja, its twin towers linked by a bridge and a restaurant that was supposed to rotate (but didn't). Still further out, in Zemun, is the once-glamorous **Hotel Yugoslavia**, a 1969 luxury development where both Queen Elizabeth II and Richard Nixon both stayed. It was targeted by NATO in 1999 on account of notorious paramilitary leader Arkan using one wing as a base.

Genex Tower

twentieth- and twenty-first-century works, the collection straddling pre- and post-war Yugoslav art, from surrealism and socialist art to the avant-garde. The performance art of perhaps Serbia's most famous living artist, Marina Abramović, is also showcased; fittingly, a couple of performance artists wearing masks of Serbian President Alexander Vučić were arrested at the museum's 2017 reopening following a decade-long refurb. Outside, there's a sculpture park.

COMMUNIST-ERA ARCHITECTURE

Stretching deep into the New Belgrade hinterland from here are the famous residential *blokovi* ('the blocks'), post-war Yugoslav-era apartment buildings divided into 70 blocks. They are numbered – somewhat confusingly – by the order in which they were built, rather than by location. Building work on the Communists' new city across the Sava – intended to be a workers' utopia, with homes that would flatten out class privilege and bring a decent standard of living to all – began in 1947, with work brigades of volunteer workers and students laying the first foundations.

A number of notable examples of utopian post-war architecture are scattered across New Belgrade (see box, page 78). They are geographically dispersed, and several can be admired only from the outside, so scouting them out independently on foot or via a series of buses may be a bit much for any but the most dedicated enthusiasts. However, excellent guided tours taking in the main Yugoslav-era sites are run by both YugoTour (from inside a clapped-out old Zastava) and from a bike saddle with iBikeBelgrade (see page 114).

New Belgrade is inextricably associated with the post-war era, but 1945 was not year zero here. Construction began on this side

JUDENLAGER SEMLIN

In December 1941, the Old Exhibition Ground's pavilions were converted to create *Judenlager Semlin* (Semlin being the German name for Zemun): a concentration camp in which the city's remaining Jewish population of some 7,000 people, as well as Roma, were interned. In the spring of 1942, records show that approximately 6,300 Jewish inmates were killed here in mobile gas vans. Known euphemistically in German as a 'delousing truck' (*Entlausungswagen*), these were normal trucks whose exhaust pipe was diverted to release the fumes into the sealed compartment at the back. Within a 15-minute trip, 100 passengers would die of carbon monoxide poisoning. In less than two months, two junior SS officers took 65–70 trips to Jajinci, a village by mount Avala, south of the city, killing thousands of people on the journey; on arrival, their victims were buried in mass graves. With Belgrade's Jewish population decimated, Semlin lager became after 1942 the main transit camp for political prisoners being moved on to eastern Europe.

Holocaust memorial

of the Sava in the final decade before World War II, as the population of Belgrade continued to grow. Located south of Brankov bridge, between the Ušće shopping centre and the river, **Staro Sajmište** ❸ (the Old Exhibition Ground) was built in 1937 for industrial fairs, exhibitions and sporting events. This cluster of neglected buildings and overgrown grass is today a poor residential area; but during the war, when the west bank of the Sava was part of the NDH governed by Croatia's fascist Ustaše, it witnessed one of the darkest chapters of Belgrade's troubled twentieth-century history.

Just by the Sava River, a hulking bronze statue erected in 1995 resembling a split circle marks a **Holocaust memorial** commemorating those who died at Staro Sajmište. But although there has been talk of a memorial complex here for years, a 'Serbian Yad Vashem' even, nothing has yet been done to adequately mark the fact that this is a former concentration camp. The site is inhabited; laundry dries in the breeze; there is even a restaurant and a sports ground, where children take part in football training. With no way of 'officially' visiting Staro Sajmište, probably the most sensitive way to recognize its past – with the least associated risk of upsetting current residents – is to take part in a curated guided tour via YugoTour or iBikeBelgrade, some of which include this area (see page 114).

ZEMUN

Further northwest along the Danube (a short hop by bus or taxi from New Belgrade's waterfront) is Zemun, which has the feel of a charming and sleepy backwater set against the hustle of central Belgrade. For almost two centuries, from 1717 until World War I, it was held by the Austro-Hungarian Empire. Until the late nineteenth century, with the Ottomans occupying Kalemegdan on the Sava's east bank, two monumental continental empires stared each other out here – with only the aptly named Great War Island to divide them.

After World War I, with Ottomans and Austrians convincingly ejected from the region, Zemun was integrated into the capital of the new Yugoslav kingdom. But during World War II, the old fault-line was resurrected as the Danube and Sava rivers again divided two sides: this time, Serbia proper (under Nazi occupation) faced Croatia's Ustaša government, which occupied Zemun.

Today, people come to Zemun principally for the pedestrianized waterfront, known as **Zemun quay** (Zemunski kej, officially Kej oslobodjenja, liberation quay). Here on the riverside promenade, perhaps more than anywhere else in Belgrade, you get a real feel for the vastness of the Danube. Lining the quay are restaurants and cafés specializing mainly in seafood, with outdoor seating affording stunning river views. A lunch at one of the fish restaurants – particularly

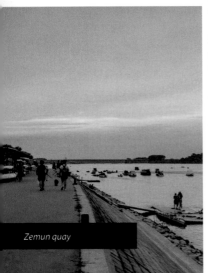

Zemun quay

Шаран (Šaran; see page 111)
– is a true rite in Belgrade life.

Away from the riverside, on
Gardoš Hill is the 1896 **Gardoš
Tower** ㉞, also known as the
Tower of Sibinjanin Janko or
the Millennium Tower (daily
10am–7pm). The views of
both New and 'Old' Belgrade
are rightly feted. The tower
was built to commemorate
one thousand years since the
Hungarians had arrived to the
Pannonian plain in 896 AD;

The Zemun Clan

In the late 1990s and early
2000s, Zemun was known
as a mafia heartland. The
'Zemun Clan' ruled the
roost, with a predilection for
mobster nicknames such as
'The Rat', 'The Cheat', and
'Bugsy'. In 2003, the gang
assassinated Prime Minister
Zoran Djindjić, and a
crackdown soon followed.

Zemun was the southernmost point of the Austro-Hungarian Empire's
territories in the late 19th century, and so received one of four towers
built at each extremity of the Empire.

ADA CIGANLIJA

If in Belgrade during the summer, and looking for a beach with
a party vibe, you could do worse than join the hordes on **Ada
Ciganlija** ㉟ (tel: 011-785 7220; www.adaciganlija.rs). Known
fondly by Belgraders as 'Ada', the island lies between the east and
west banks of the Sava. Its beach stretches for 4km (2.5 miles), with
sporting activities on offer including cycling on well laid-out tracks,
volleyball (on sand and concrete) and boat hire. For something less
strenuous, head to the beer garden, with outdoor tables and music
run by the organizers of the Belgrade Beer Festival (weekends in
June–Aug, Mon–Fri 4pm–midnight, Sat–Sun noon–midnight; check
for this year's plans on the official Ada Ciganlija website, above). To
get there, take city bus 37 from Trg Republike (Republic Square).

Belgrade has a lively after-hours scene

THINGS TO DO

NIGHTLIFE

The all-night **floating clubs** *(splavovi)* dotted along the Sava and Danube riverfronts are probably the most distinctive aspect of Belgrade nightlife, but the options for going 'out-out' have diversified hugely in recent years, from the warehouse clubs of gritty **Savamala** to the characterful bars of **Dorćol** and **Vračar**. The city is now peppered with independent, alternative places to discover, and the latest hotspot for hipster creatives – a courtyard complex set on the site of a former brewery at **Cetinjska 15** – is conveniently close to the heart of the Old Town (just around the corner from Skadarlija).

Big nights out start late here (clubs open from midnight or 2am and typically close at 5am), but if you head out for a post-work or pre-dinner drink at 5–6pm or cocktails at 8pm, you won't be alone.

BARS

OLD TOWN

Amélie *Topličin Venac 4*. This snug café-bar on pedestrianized, sloping Topličin Venac has a quirky interior featuring Singer sewing machine tables and a traditional Serbian stove. In the evenings, patrons spill out onto the outdoor terrace, lit by fairy lights. The name (inspired by the 2001 Audrey Tautou film) is a nod to the fond idea that the 'three crescents' area is Belgrade's Montmartre. Sun–Thurs 10am–midnight, Fri & Sat till 1am.

Black Turtle II *Kosančićev Venac 30*; www.theblackturtle.com. One of a long-established Belgrade chain, *Black Turtle II* boasts a picture-pretty location – its terrace on cobbled Kosančićev Venac

Wise words at Cetinjska 15

overlooks the Sava, with vistas across to New Belgrade. The basement has a cosy, slightly grungy feel. Try the Rauchbier or fruit beers from the Black Turtle brewery in a Vojvodina village. Sun–Thurs 9am–midnight, Fri & Sat 9am till 1am.

Druid *Cincer Janka 1*; tel: 11-218 1540. Secluded drinking den tucked away down a small street. There is no sign at the door that suggests it is a cocktail bar, but descend to the basement and you'll discover inventive mixologists that create miracles in a glass. The small space fills up quickly, so make a reservation in advance to nab a table. Sun–Thurs 5pm–midnight, Fri & Sat till 1am.

Jazz Bašta *Male Stepenice 1a*. There's live jazz in this intimate little wine bar decked out with French-style decor. Patrons huddle round small tables, up close to whoever's playing that night. Entry fee around €2 for music nights. Best reached by heading down Male stepenice ('the small staircase') from Kosančićev venac. Thurs–Sun 5pm–1am.

Dorćol

Blaznavac *Knejinje Ljubice 18*. A characterful cocktail bar easily spotted from the street by the neon daubed onto the historic facades. Its courtyard features a vintage nineteenth-century coach, a gigantic papier-mâché elephant, and busts of the eponymous Blaznavac – an obscure nineteenth-century politician. For chillier nights, there are outdoor heaters and mulled wine or 'sumadiski čaj' on offer. Sun–Thurs 9am–1am, Fri & Sat till 2am.

Endorfin Gastro-pub *Braće Jugovića 3*; www.endorfin-bar-restaurant.business.site. A sizeable, slightly macho bar-eatery in Dorćol laying claim to be Serbia's first gastropub. Range of craft beers and good international grub (truffle fries, Philly cheese steak, steak tartare); food pairings and tasting sessions can be reserved for groups (tel: 011-328 1701). Mon–Thurs 1pm–midnight, Fri & Sat till 1am.

Exploring the city on two wheels

Pastis *Strahinjica Bana 52b*. A little slice of Parisian life, *Pastis* has held its own in a fast-changing Dorćol scene with its effective and understated formula: a civilized bistro-bar with corner seating, soft lighting and an extensive wine list, including champagne. Daily 8am–12.30am.

Wider city centre

Centrala Bar *Bulevar Zorana Đinđića 106a*. One of those unpretentious Belgrade café-pubs that shifts seamlessly from good food and afternoon coffees to buzzy evening drinks. Inside, *Centrala* is all dark wood and bare brick, set to a soundtrack of DJs and live music. There are live game broadcasts too. Great atmosphere. Daily 8am–1am.

Samo Pivo! *Milutina Bojica 2, just off Balkanska 13*. A sociable, noisy beer hall with a student ambience around the corner from *Hotel*

Samo Pivo!, or 'Just Beer'

Moskva. The name means 'Just Beer', and Samo Pivo delivers to the brief, with a good mix of keenly priced Balkan and international options (Russian, Belgian, Japanese). Head up the grotty-looking steps from Balkanska to the first floor. Sun–Fri noon–midnight, Fri & Sat till 1am.

O.U.R. Pub *Beogradska 71*; www.ourpub.rs. Close to St Mark's Church, this place is a hybrid between an old man's pub and a modern brewery/taproom. It's the ideal locale if you're looking to put away volumes of Czech, Slovene and regional beers, with a litre costing just under €3. Hosts regular music nights and televised sports. Mon–Thurs 8am–midnight, Fri & Sat till 2am, Sun 10am–midnight.

World Travellers' Club *Klub Svetskih Putnika, Bulevar despota Stefana 7*; www.clubsvetskihputnika.business.site. A 'living room bar' packed with personality, founded in 1999 for internationally minded friends to get together. It remains a haven for the weary globetrotter, all cosy nooks and clusters of eclectic decor, including vintage clocks, maps and photographs of old Belgrade. Look for the *Klub Svetskih Putnika* sign above an apartment block gate at no.7; buzz for Klub and once admitted, go through the dimly lit entrance hall and downstairs. Daily 9am–2am.

Vračar

Kultura *Kralja Milutina 4*. Relaxed, bijou cocktail bar serving up creations with names to conjure with, from Penicillin to Skylark Sparkle. Punters nestle up against the bar to watch the expert mixologists at work. Sun–Thurs 9am–midnight, Fri–Sat 9am till 1am.

CLUBS

The legal drinking age in Serbia is 18, but many clubs won't admit under-21s, and most venues will not admit anyone who seems excessively drunk. Clubs get launched, close down and move fairly often, so check clubs' websites and (more often actively updated)

Facebook pages before planning your night. Most of the clubs on board *splavovi* (floating lounges) are open May to September only.

Drugstore *Bulevar Despota Stefana 115*; www.drugstorebeograd. com. At the sharper end of Belgrade's clubbing scene is *Drugstore*, a vast techno warehouse set in a former slaughterhouse a way out of town (hitching a cab is advisable). The cavernous interior features blaring red lights, a 'brutal' aesthetic and an intense atmosphere. Fri & Sat, 11pm–10am.

Hua Hua *Ada Ciganlija*. Established since 1983, the *Hua Hua* – named after a Dutch ship – is a floating riverboat hangout usually packed wall-to-wall with attractive partygoers and celebrities. The vibe is lively, the music courtesy of live bands; it's a great spot for fans of folk tunes. Popular so make a reservation well ahead. Fri & Sat midnight–5am.

Downtown Belgrade

Hype *Karadjordjeva 46*; www.hypebelgrade.com. Reliable, mainstream club in Savamala with varied music nights ranging from retro pop classics to hip-hop, r'n'b and electronica. A pumping sound system and relentless strobes crank up the atmosphere. Minimum age 23; dress code smart-casual. Wed–Sat midnight–4.30am.

Klub 20/44 *Ušće bb*. Named after Belgrade's geographical coordinates, *20/44* is a *splav* that runs year-round. Set on the Sava River (round the curve as you walk south towards Brankov bridge), it has a more free-spirited vibe than some of the more 'see-and-be-seen' *splavovi*, and regularly hosts local DJs such as Tijana T. Through the spring and summer seasons, guests dance on the deck against a backdrop of stunning river views: twinkling lights, sunset and sunrise all in one night. In the colder months, the action moves below deck. Entry costs around €5. Fri & Sat 11pm–4am.

Mladost/Ludost/Gadost *Karadjordjeva 44*; www.mladost-ludost. com. Concentrated on one site in the former industrial area of Savamala is this series of interconnecting bars and clubs: *Mladost* (meaning "youth"), *Ludost* ("madness"), and shiny newcomer *Gadost* ("nastiness" or "disgust"). All with industrial-chic interiors, they've nailed the Savamala brand of edgy cool. *Gadost* is increasingly the place for Belgrade's most epic after-parties, open until 7am at weekends. *Ludost* Fri & Sat midnight–5am, Sun–Thurs 10pm–4am; *Mladost* Fri & Sat 10pm–4am; *Gadost* Thurs 10pm–4am, Fri & Sat 11pm–7am.

Sprat *Cetinjska 15*. Not a small herring but a hipsterish first-floor bar-club hosting local bands and DJ sets. The name just means 'floor', and there's a refreshingly unselfconscious, inclusive approach to a night out here, with the Serbian craft beers flowing and eclectic music acts coming thick and fast. Sun–Thurs 5pm–midnight, Fri & Sat till 1am.

Zaokret *Cetinjska 15*. Perhaps Belgraders' favourite Cetinjska venue, *Zaokret* exists somewhere at the interface between a bar and a club.

The elegant Hotel Moskva café

Creative types come here for the ever-changing calendar of gigs and DJ nights, ramshackle decor and bohemian atmosphere. Not a bad choice for afternoon coffee either – check out those homemade brownies. Sun–Thurs 10am–midnight, Fri & Sat till 1am.

SWEET TREATS

Parallel to the rise of craft breweries in Belgrade has been the rise of artisanal patisseries and gelaterias. It's welcome news for those with a sweet tooth.

Bacio Gelato *Višnjićeva 10 and Njegoševa 1a*; www.baciogelato. rs. Delectable, locally made gelato in both Dorćol (Višnjićeva) and Vračar (Njegoševa) locations. Founded in 2009, *Bacio* supplies ice-creams to bars and cafés across the city; options include vegan options and miniature ice-cream cakes. A must-try. Daily 9am–midnight.

Ferdinand Knedle *Cara Lazara 19*; www.ferdinandknedle.hr. A steady stream of Belgraders flocks to this little dumpling emporium at all hours of the day and evening for sweet and savoury goodies to eat in or snaffle at home. With Portuguese tiles and uplighting, the interiors ensure no Belgrade hipster would blush to be seen here. Daily 10am–11pm.

Hotel Moskva cakes *Balkanska 1*; www.hotelmoskva.rs. Suffused with old-world charm, the *Hotel Moskva*'s ground floor café continues to attract well-heeled older Belgraders as well as visitors who want to enjoy the finer things in life. With views over Terazije, it is an ideal spot for mulling over the day's papers while listening to the resident pianist. Try sumptuous sundaes or the house speciality, the Moscow Schnitte. Daily 7am–midnight.

Luff Gelato *Prote Mateja 30, Vračar*; www.luffgelato.business.site. On the corner with Njegoševa, this glass-panelled parlour serves delicious, locally made gelato. Try the raspberry flavour in honour of one of Serbia's biggest food exports. New seasonal concoctions appear every few weeks. Daily 8am–10pm.

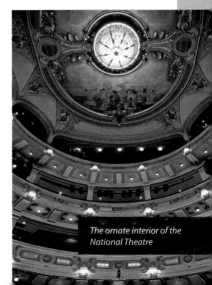
The ornate interior of the National Theatre

Mandarina cake shop *Gračanička 16*; www.mandarinacakeshop.rs. Tiny, elegant café, with just a few tables inside and out, offering exquisite cake creations. Try the raw chocolate cheesecake or the raspberry bombe – no regrets. Daily 9am–8pm.

Fresh produce for sale at Kalenic Pijaca

ENTERTAINMENT

Serbia has a strong 'high culture' heritage from Yugoslavia, when the arts were well respected and well supported; there are full programmes year-round at a number of theatres and concert halls. The range of contemporary live music on offer is huge, from gigs in stadiums to DJ nights in bars and clubs.

CLASSICAL MUSIC, THEATRE AND OPERA

Two major classical music venues are centrally located on Studentski Trg: **Kolarac Hall** (*Studentski Trg 5*; tel: 011-263 0550, www.kolarac.rs) and the **Belgrade Philharmonic Orchestra** (*Studentski Trg 11*; tel: 011-328 2977, www.bgf.rs). A more mixed programme, featuring both classical and contemporary music, is on offer at New Belgrade's popular **Sava Centre** (*Milentija Popovica 9*; tel: 011-220 6060, www.savacentar.net). Major gigs by international artists usually take place at the city's main stadium, the **Štark Arena** (*Bulevar Arsenija Čarnojevića 58*; tel: 011-220 2222, www.starkarena.co.rs).

The **National Theatre** on Trg Republike (*Francuska 3*; tel: 011-262 0946, www.narodnopozoriste.rs) is over 150 years old and stages opera, ballet and theatre productions. The **Yugoslav Drama Theatre** in Vračar (*Kralja Milana 50*; tel: 011-306 1957, www.jdp.rs) puts on a mixture of classics and modern work (occasionally with English surtitles).

LIVE MUSIC BARS

Jazz-lovers will adore the up-close acoustics of **Jazz Bašta**. For indie/alternative music, look out for upcoming gigs on the websites of **Zaokret** (www.kisobran.org) and **KC Grad** (www.kcgrad.rs). See page 85 for more information on nightlife.

SHOPPING

The pedestrianized **Knez Mihailova** is lined by a range of well-known international brands and more exclusive boutiques, should you need to top up your wardrobe while in Belgrade. The glossy **Rajićeva** mall (*Kneza Mihaila 54*; www.rajicevashoppingcenter.rs; daily 10am–10pm), right in the centre of the Old Town, has (mainly high-end) European fashion brands, plus a handy minimarket and pharmacy in the basement. The New Belgrade equivalent is **Ušće**, Serbia's largest mall (*Bulevar Mihajla Pupina 4*; www.usceshopping-center.rs; daily 10am–10pm).

Shopping in Belgrade can, however, be more interesting than this. A number of independent outlets sell souvenirs and gifts that reflect the city's originality and creativity, while the city's markets are a great place to pick up fresh produce sourced from the surrounding countryside.

SOUVENIRS AND GIFTS

Bosiljčić *Gavrila Principa 14*. A tiny, family-run sweet shop selling *ratluk* (Turkish delight) and a small selection of other candies made using traditional methods. In business since 1936, the store is more authentic than it is glossy. Find it close to Zeleni venac (see Markets, opposite).

Parfimerija Sava *Kralja Petra 75*. Serbia was a centre of perfume-making in the 1950s; now just one store remains. Founded in 1954, Parfimerija Sava is as evocative as it is fragrant. The owner, son of the founder, mixes perfumes to customers' specifications, wielding large, hand-labelled glass bottles and giant atomizers to get the perfect mix. It's very reasonably priced: around €20 for 30ml of perfume; €10 for 50ml of cologne.

Museum of Yugoslavia shop *Mihaila Mike Jankovića 6*. The best place to buy kitsch and possibly only half-ironic items of Yugonostalgia: fridge magnets, mugs and t-shirts emblazoned with Tito's face and the old Yugo car.

Rakia & Co *Terazije 42, Njegoševa 32b*. Quaffable souvenirs, chocolates and interesting books, including the excellent *Snippets of Serbia* (see page 119).

Tricikl *Francuska 5*; www.tricikl.rs. A Dorćol boutique selling cool, contemporary Serbian-made items, from chunky wooden jewellery to artisanal chocolates, and beard elixir to bow ties.

SHOPPING PHRASES

How much is this? **Koliko ovo košta?**

Do you take credit cards? **Primate li kreditne kartice?**

Can you change … money/pounds/dollars/euros for me? **Možete li promeniti novac/funti sterlinga/dolara/evra za mene?**

Where is there a cash machine? **Gde je bankomat?**

Red Star in action

Vina Srbije *Zmaja od Noćaja 9*; www.vinoivinogradarstvo.net. Wine shop in the heart of Dorćol selling Serbian, Montenegrin and Croatian bottles. Knowledgeable staff can brief you on regional vintners and grape varieties.

MARKETS

Visiting one of Belgrade's lively **food markets** is an affordable way to pick up fresh fruit and veg; jars of local honey or *ajvar* make great presents. It's also a great way to get a flavour of Serbian life beyond the Belgrade bubble.

Kalenic Pijaca *eastern end of Njegoševa in Vračar*. A covered market selling fresh, seasonal produce sourced from the surrounding villages. From 6am daily.

Zeleni Venac *junction of Kraljice Natalije with Brankov bridge*. Descend the steps from Brankov bridge into Zeleni Venac and take in the sheer abundance of this central market: fruit and vegetables

Football matches can be tense affairs

piled high, alongside jars of homemade sauces and pickles, honey and freshly picked herbs. From 6am daily.

SPECTATOR SPORTS

FOOTBALL

Belgrade's biggest football teams are Red Star (Crvena Zvezda – they play in red and white, and their supporters are known as the heroes, Delije) and Partizan (who play in black and white, their supporters known as the gravediggers, Grobari). Even though their stadiums are located side by side in the Dedinje area, the two teams are the fiercest of rivals. The derby between the two teams is known as the 'Eternal Derby', Večiti derbi, and derby matches are often noisy and chaotic, with flares, missiles, violence and arrests frequent occurrences. You can book tickets in advance for Red

Star's Rajko Mitic Stadium (informally known as the Marakana) at Ljutice Bogdana 1a (tel: 011-206 7773, www.crvenazvezdafk.com) and for the Partizan Stadium at Humska 1a (tel: 011-369 3815; www.partizan.co.rs).

BASKETBALL

Both Red Star and Partizan are part of multisport clubs, which means there are Red Star and Partizan teams competing in a variety of sports such as basketball, volleyball and waterpolo. In basketball, Serbia is one of the world's leading nations, beating the mighty USA in the 2019 World Cup. To catch one of the regular games between Partizan, Red Star or other professional teams, you can buy tickets a couple of days before the game at the Aleksandar Nikolić Hall, popularly known as Pionir Hall, which is part of Tašmajdan Sports Centre (*Čarlija Čaplina 39*; tel: 011-655 6501, www.tasmajdan.rs).

FOOTBALL AND POLITICS

Both Red Star and Partizan football teams were founded in 1945. Red Star started life as an anti-fascist youth society, while Partizan was founded by officers from the Yugoslav Army. During the conflict in Bosnia in 1992–95, Red Star fans were linked to nationalist paramilitaries operating in Bosnia, in particular to Arkan's Tigers (formally the Serbian Volunteer Guard), one of the most famous and brutal of the paramilitaries, which was founded from among the *Delije* or Heroes (Red Star 'ultras'). The link between football hooliganism, 'ultras' and Serb nationalism has continued: in 2019, Red Star caused a stir by arranging an unsanctioned football match in the (disputed) majority-Serb northern region of Kosovo, and faced an international ban for racist chants.

BELGRADE FOR CHILDREN

Whilst the traffic and walking distances may be a little forbidding for very young children, Belgrade is a great place to visit with older children. The **Botanical Gardens** (see page 62) are lovely to explore (look out for the bug hotel), while almost every city park (including Tašmajdan, Kalemegdan and Friendship Park in New Belgrade) includes a playground. In the 'Montmartre' area, look out for the little playground by the Vojvoda Vuk statue in **Proleće Park**: well situated to pop into Ferdinand Knedle (see page 93) afterwards for a dumpling and a hot chocolate. Older children will also enjoy a visit to the **Automobile Museum** (see page 60) and the interactive experiments at the **Nikola Tesla Museum** (see page 65).

While the **Belgrade Zoo** (see page 43) on the Kalemegdan site is sometimes touted as a family-friendly activity, there is a sad feeling (and odour) to the place. More fun is **staying on a floating raft** on the Danube, such as ArkaBarka (see page 140), and eating out at nearby **Keops** (pancake nirvana; see page 111). If in Dorćol, **Red Bread** (see page 108) is an ideal dining spot when you have young ones in tow, with its children's menu (think meatballs and pasta), play table with crayons, and baby-changing facilities – all unusual for Belgrade.

Botanical Gardens

WHAT'S ON

January: Orthodox Christmas Eve (6 January): *Badnji Dan* (named after the *badnjak* or oak branch) is commemorated with public bonfires, the largest being outside St Sava's Church. Orthodox Christmas Day (7 January): families celebrate with pork roasts and the breaking of *česnica*, a beautifully decorated bread with a coin hidden inside.

February: FEST International Film Festival, in late February to early March, showcases new releases in world cinema (www.fest.rs).

April: The No Sleep Festival (www.nosleepfestival.com) is a thumping mix of techno, electronica and house – a spin-off to the summer EXIT Festival.

May: The Belgrade Marathon (www.bdgmarathon.org) lures runners to the city's streets. Orthodox Easter (April or May) is marked with church services, egg-painting and egg-cracking fun. Enjoy late-night cultural escapades until midnight on Museum Night (www.nocmuzeja.rs).

June: The Tour de Serbie bike race kicks off in Belgrade. BELEF – the Belgrade summer festival – runs from late June to early July, bringing with it outdoor theatre and concerts, some inside Kalemegdan Fortress (www.belef.rs).

July: EXIT Festival, a major music festival attracting around 200,000 revellers, is held annually at Petrovaradin Fortress in Novi Sad, an hour's drive north of Belgrade (www.exitfest.org).

August: Belgrade Beer Festival, a five-day extravaganza of local, regional and world beers coupled with music, is staged in Friendship Park (www.belgradebeerfest.com). Guča trumpet festival, in western Serbia, is a heady combination of brass orchestras, grilled meats and *rakija* (www.guca.rs).

September: BITEF International Theatre Festival takes place in performance spaces across Belgrade (www.bitef.rs).

October: Belgrade Jazz Festival is marked by concerts across the city (www.bjf.rs).

November: Classical music at Belgrade Music Festival (www.bemus.rs).

December: Christmas Market ('Open Heart Square') held on Trg Republike, with wooden stalls selling traditional craft goods, mulled wine and merry-go-rounds. New Year's Eve: free concerts and fireworks at Trg Republike; parties on the riverside *splavovi* (best booked in advance).

FOOD AND DRINK

SERBIAN CUISINE

Serbs recognize the value of food as an important aspect of their cultural heritage, and Serbian cuisine remains well represented in Belgrade's restaurant scene. Grilled meats are the cornerstone of national fare, with supporting roles for traditional salads such as *šopska salata* and *ajvar* and home-baked breads such as cornbread (*proja*). As Rebecca West penned in her 1942 travel memoir *Black Lamb and Grey Falcon*: "We ate too large a lunch, as is apt to be one's habit in Belgrade, if one is man enough to stand up to peasant food made luxurious by urban opulence of supply." One thing is certain: you will not go hungry here.

WHEN TO EAT

Breakfast is usually rushed and stodgy, with queues at city bakeries for a slice of *burek* and a yoghurt to wash it down with. Weekday lunches are fitted into the working day, but weekend lunches remain traditionally taken at leisure and at length, kicking off as late as 2–3pm, with large groups of family or friends. Dinner out usually starts around 8.30pm.

Food hero

The 'karadjordje schnitzel' – a dish inspired by a liberation hero (see page 19) – is a modern classic of Serbian cuisine, invented in 1959 for a visiting Soviet dignitary. A pork or veal steak is rolled into a sausage shape, encased in breadcrumbs, and filled with *kajmak* (cream cheese).

WHAT TO EAT

On the **meat** front, Serbian specialities include *ćevapčići*, fingers of grilled meat served with onions, and *pljeskavica*, an (often vast) circular meat patty made of a mix of ground beef, pork and lamb. To call it a 'patty' or 'burger' seems too pedestrian; a *pljeskavica*'s flavour far outdoes that of its American cousin. Other meaty treats include *ražnjići* (kebab skewers of grilled pork or veal) and the gut-busting Karadjordje schnitzel, or *Karadjordjeva šnicla*. If you're dining by the Danube, it's well worth trying *riblja corba* (fish soup), spiced with paprika and glowing red.

Ćevapčići

The majority of Serbian land is still given over to agricultural production, and most restaurants offer an abundance of **salads**, from *šopska salata* (tomato, cucumber, onion, peppers and salty cheese) to pastes such as red-pepper *ajvar* and spicy garlic-and-pepper *lutenica*. A 'salad' such as *ajvar* is usually served in a relatively small portion; take a *mezze* approach and you'll have more than enough sustenance.

Bread comes in several satisfying varieties: *lepinja* (a puffed-up bun, which like pitta bread separates into two layers during baking), *proja* (a cornbread, excellent with cheese), and *devrek* (bread rings coated in sesame seeds). Festive bakes include exquisitely decorated *slavski kolač* (slava bread), topped with wreaths, crosses and flowers, and eaten to celebrate a family's saint's day, and *česnica* – a Christmas bread with knots and plaits baked into the design and a coin hidden inside.

Pastry is also an important pillar of Serbian cuisine, and the classic snack or breakfast food here is *burek* bought from a bakery: a

Burek is a breakfast treat

flaky pastry filled with soft cheese or minced beef with onions, served with a pot of runny yoghurt on the side. On the dairy front, do sample *kajmak*, a salty clotted cream used both as a snack (with bread) and as an ingredient.

Vegan food is increasingly fashionable in trendy quarters of Belgrade, as is artisanal gelato (see page 92). Brunch is growing in popularity too, often with an Anglo-American twist: think omelettes, smoothies, granola and eggs Benedict. Italian and international cuisine (pizzas, pastas, salads) are widely available, and dished up pretty much anywhere that isn't specifically a Serbian restaurant.

DRINKS

The local drinks menu can and does often run to many pages. Traditionally, Serbia's drink of choice is *rakija* (or *rakia*), a strong fruit-based brandy (40 percent proof upward, usually higher if homemade) based on a range of fruits: most commonly plums (to create *šljivovica*), but also quince (*dunjica*), apricots (*kajsija*) and others. If you need a warming hot toddy in winter, try *šumadijski čaj* or 'Šumadija tea': hot boiled *rakia*. For a more mellow occasion, Serbia and neighbouring Montenegro produce a number of good wines, notably Prokupac (Serbian red), Vranac (Montenegrin red) and Serbia's aromatic Tamjanika, named after 'tamjan' (frankincense), and similar to a Muscat. The local craft beer scene has rocketed, with Kabinet, Salto and Dogma the key Serbian brands to look out for. *Živeli* (cheers)!

SERBIAN SPECIALITIES

ajvar roast pepper *(pimento)* spread

baklava sweet pastry with chopped nuts and honey

burek filo pastry filled with meat, soft cheese or spinach

ćevapi (ćevapčići) meat rissoles

đuveč thick meat and vegetable stew (the 'đ' sound is pronounced 'dj').

gulaš goulash (paprika-spiced meat stew)

kajmak salted clotted cream/soft cheese

karađorđeva fine rolled-up steak (the 'đ' sound is pronounced 'dj').

kashkaval yellow cheese

kiseli kupus pickled cabbage

kobasice sausages, usually spicy

mućkalica spicy stew of pork, tomatoes and peppers

palačinke pancakes

pljeskavica minced beef or pork burger/patty

pogača bread baked in the ashes of the fireplace and then the oven

popara sturdy breakfast dish of bread, milk, cheese

prebranac bean soup

proja cornbread

riblja čorba fish stew

sarma cabbage leaf parcels of meat and rice

srpska salata salad with tomato, onion, cucumber

šopska salata like *srpska salata* but with white cheese on top

sudžuk dried, smoked beef sausage

svadbarski kupus 'wedding cabbage': cabbage with pork or mutton, slow-cooked

IN THE RESTAURANT

A table for … one person/two people, please **Molim sto za jedno/dvoje**

TO HELP YOU TO ORDER…

Can I look at the menu, please? **Mogu li dobiti jelovnik?**

I'm vegetarian **Ja sam vegetarijanac** (men) **or Ja sam vegetarijanka** (women)

I'm vegan **Vegan sam**

I'd like … **Želim….**

The bill, please **Račun, molim**

FOOD BASICS…

apple **jabuka**
beans **pasulj**
bread **hleb**
cheese **sir**
chicken **piletina**
dish of the day **jelo dana**
fish **riba**

garlic **beli luk**
grilled meat **jela sa roštilja**
ice cream **sladoled**
meat **meso**
potatoes **krompir**
raspberries **maline**
vegetables **povrće**

STYLE …

boiled **baren**
fried **prženo**

from the grill **sa roštilja**
roast **pečeno**

DRINKS …

wine (homemade/red/white) **vino (domaće/crno/belo)**
water (mineral/sparkling) **voda (mineralna/gazirana)**
(not) tap water **(A ne) vode iz slavine**
beer **pivo**
coffee **kafa**
tea (with milk/with lemon) **čaj (sa mlekom/sa limunom)**

WHERE TO EAT

We have used the following symbols to give an idea of the price for a three-course meal for one, including wine and service:

€€€€	**over 40 euros**
€€€	**25–40 euros**
€€	**15–25 euros**
€	**below 15 euros**

SKADARLIJA

Skadarlija remains the go-to destination for the foolproof combination of hearty Serbian fare and traditional music performed by 'tambura orchestras' (folk bands) touring the tables. The following restaurants are the pick of the bunch; avoid being lured in by a street tout promoting lesser imitators.

Dva Jelena €€€ *Skadarska 32, tel: 011-723 4885;* www.dvajelena.rs. Not just for tourists, *Dva Jelena* ('Two Deer') was founded in 1832 and retains its old-world charm, as well as its authentic popularity with locals. Its traditional dark-wood interiors are an atmospheric setting for folk singers wielding accordions. Come here to defy the troubles of the world and revel in an excess of meat (try the tender, juicy pork *ražnjići*), wine and song. Daily 10am–1am.

Supermarket Deli €€ *Topličin Venac 19–21, tel: 011-202 8008;* www.supermarketdeli.rs. A fashionable canteen-deli set on picturesque Topličin Venac, serving an excellent range of brunch and breakfast goodies, plus filling salads and sandwiches. Boost your vitamin quotient with a green smoothie (apple, kiwi, parsley and lettuce) or superfood salad. Mon–Fri 8am–midnight, Sat & Sun 9am–midnight.

Tri Šešira €€€ *Skadarska 29, tel: 011-724 7501;* www.trisesira.rs. The Skadarlija essentials are done well at long-standing punters' favourite 'Three Hats': energetic folk music, grilled meats, good wine. A great introduction to the rough charms of traditional Serbian dining – though you do pay a premium for eating on the main tourist drag. Daily 11am–2pm.

DORĆOL

Drama ćevapi € *Dositejeva 7a, tel: 011-408 4035*. Bang-up fast food in a trendy industrial-chic setting, with the mandatory exposed brickwork and filament light bulbs. The menu is focused exclusively on *ćevapi*, served in helpings of one (for the abstemious), five or ten, alongside a *lepinja* roll, spicy *ajvar*, *kajmak* and onions. Take away or eat in. Mon–Thurs 9am–11pm, Fri & Sat till 3am.

Iva New Balkan Cuisine €€€ *Kneginje Ljubice 11, tel: 011-328 5007;* www. newbalkancuisine.com. *Iva's* philosophy is that Serbian cuisine must not stagnate; it must innovate to survive. The result is a contemporary, refined take on Balkan cuisine, with a quiet, minimalist interior putting the food centre stage. Try delectable homemade pasta with Herzegovinian cheese, charcoal-smoked aubergine, or chocolate cake with black truffles and thyme. Mon–Sat 9am–midnight, Sun till 11pm.

Red Bread €€ *Obilićev Venac 22, tel: 011-328 7159;* www.reabread.rs. Adorned with bright, cheerful retro travel posters, and with a tempting range of breakfast options (Canadian pancakes, granola with yoghurt and home-made strawberry sauce, Orange Spice smoothie), there's no better place in Dorćol to start your day with a zing. Staff are cheerful, and younger visitors are also catered for, with a children's menu and baby-changing facilities. Daily 6am–6pm.

WIDER OLD TOWN

Klub Književnika €€€€ *Writers' Club, Francuska 7, tel: 063-338 538;* www. klubknjizevnika.rs. A stalwart of the Belgrade cultural scene for over 70 years, with former patrons including Jean-Paul Sartre, Simone de Beauvoir, Richard Burton and Elizabeth Taylor, the *Writers' Club* combines exceptional food with a creative atmosphere. The roasted veal with sauerkraut, venison goulash, and fillet of Danube zander are all excellent. Service is attentive; and the Serbian wine list ensures an evening here passes in a pleasurable blur. Bosnian-born Yugoslav Ivo Andrić gave his first speech to friends here after winning the Nobel Prize for Literature in 1961. Mon–Thurs noon–midnight, Fri & Sat 10am–midnight, Sun 10am–10pm.

Mandala €€€ *Kosančićev Venac 9, tel: 011-407 9782;* www.lorca-design.com/ en/Mandala. A unique addition to the city's food scene, *Mandala* is a high-end, plant-based restaurant that uses only fresh, organic and seasonal produce in its recipes. Founded by a furniture designer-turned-shamanic healer, the inventive menu is sprinkled with lifestyle advice as well as vegan and vegetarian dishes. Truth be told, there's a risk of style over substance, but the food is perfectly palatable, and staff are charming. Sample dishes include Inka Warrior smoothie and carrot lox tartine. Sun–Thurs 9am–midnight, Fri & Sat till 1am.

Manufaktura €€€ *Kralja Petra 13, tel: 011-218 0044;* www.restoran-manufaktura.rs/en. This easy-going beer hall and food canteen is well suited to large groups or stag parties, with its contemporary vibe, super-speedy service and fantastic central location, just off Knez Mihailova. The emphasis is on sampling elements of Serbian and regional cuisine without the traditional ceremony of a deeply involved three-course meal. Highlights from the menu include Vojvodina goulash and imperial meat (a smoked pork steak). Spot the restaurant by the cluster of upside-down red umbrellas hanging outside. Daily 9am–midnight.

WIDER CITY CENTRE

Bistro Mali Pijac €€ *Karadjordjeva 61, tel: 069-777 989;* www.bistromalipijac. rs. Civilized and spacious corner bistro in Savamala, close by the Belgrade Waterfront development. Ideal for brunch (such as omelette with mushrooms and goat's cheese) or, later in the day, lingering over a large glass of red. Mon–Thurs 9am–11pm, Fri & Sun till 1am.

Majstor and Margarita €€ *Balkanska 16, tel: 060-480 8621;* www.majstori-margarita.rs. Intimate little independent pizzeria (its name a pizza-based pun on Bulgakov's magic realist classic, *The Master and Margarita*) offering doughy Neapolitan-style pizzas in a fresh, pretty setting. Super-central, just off Terazije, near the Obrenović fountain. Good for families. Mon–Fri 9am–midnight, Sat & Sun 2pm–midnight.

Mezestoran Dvorište €€€ *Svetogorska 46, tel: 011-324 6515;* www.restorandvoriste.rs. This characterful Greek-themed spot is tucked away just behind the Parliament Building. It offers a wide range of Mediterranean dishes, going well beyond your standard pizza or pasta: think pork in the Ancient Greek style, Istrian beef stew, or Sultan's Delight (beef stew with aubergine purée). Enter through the residential apartment entrance; the restaurant nudges up to the back of the courtyard, with extensive indoor and outdoor seating. Daily 10am–11pm.

Znak Pitanja (?) €€ *Kafana znak pitanja, Kralja Petra 6, tel: 011-263 5421; www.znakpitanja.rs.* One of Belgrade's most famous *kafanas,* or taverns, *Znak Pitanja,* or simply *?,* gained its name ('Question Mark') following a dispute over the name which the enterprising owner resolved by adding an interrogative. Its traditional design, location and fame attract large numbers of tourists. It is undoubtedly well situated, immediately opposite the Residence of Princess Ljubica, and although the food and service lack finesse, Serbian basics (grilled pork, *ajvar*) are done well. Mon–Thurs noon–9pm, Fri–Sun 10am–10pm.

VRAČAR

Amici Restoran Pizzeria Trattoria €€ *Nebojšina 8, tel: 11-386 3999; www.amicirestoran.rs.* This popular Italian haunt is tucked away in the peace and tranquillity of Karadjordjev Park. The warm and inviting interior is dominated by wood, stone and brick, complemented by cheerful red-and-white checked tablecloths, evoking the atmosphere of an authentic trattoria. The best tables are outside in the garden overlooking the park. Mon–Sat 11am–midnight, Sun noon–6pm.

Od usta do usta € *Braće Nedić 7, tel: 061-655 0066.* This well-hidden, self-consciously cool café is set in a handy location for a laidback lunch while in Vračar. The tempting menu offers freshly made pasta and original choices such as *flammkuchen* (try the Popeye Flammkuchen with spinach, blue cheese and pear). Situated just a couple of minutes' walk from the Nikola Tesla Museum. Daily 10am–midnight.

Restoran Tri €€ *Svetogorska 46, tel: 065-333 2543; www.restorantri.com.* Style and substance combine in joyful harmony at this outstanding little Vračar restaurant. Set up by three female friends, it combines a mellow atmosphere with inventive decor and delicious food. Try the homemade ravioli in spinach sauce, pulled pork, or walnut and butter cake with craft beer truffles. To wash it all down, there's sparkling rose-petal drink or *rakija*. Mon–Thurs 11am–midnight, Fri & Sat till 1am.

Voulez-Vous €€ *Djordja Vajferta 52, tel: 011-244 0777; www.voulez-vous.rs.* A lively and sophisticated bar hidden away in a quiet residential backstreet, with a spacious terrace shaded on all sides. Off the tourist-beaten track, *Voulez-Vous* offers a fabulous range of brunch and breakfast goods (chorizo and eggs, English breakfast), cocktails and pizzas (Italian- or Chicago-style). Daily 8am–1am.

NEW BELGRADE AND ZEMUN

Keops € *Palačinkarnica Keops, Kej Oslobodjenja bb, tel: 060-037 3137; www. keops.rs.* A floating raft in New Belgrade specializing in pancakes (*palancinke*) of all shapes and sizes. Try the cherry brandy pancake with chocolate and vanilla dressing, or cheese with ham and sour cream. Popular with local families, this *splav* has a friendly, unpretentious atmosphere and food is keenly priced. Daily 9am–11pm.

Reka €€ *Kej Oslobodjenja 73b, tel: 011-261 1625; www.reka.co.rs.* A friendly family-run restaurant with few pretensions, located at the far end of the *kej* in Zemun. The bright decor, lip-smackingly good fish dishes such as *riblja corba*, and great views across the Danube make this a charming place to lunch or dine out in Zemun. Order a mulled wine (*kuvano vino*) to warm the cockles on a blustery day. Regular live music at weekends and evenings. Daily noon–2am.

Šaran €€€€ *Kej Oslobodjenja 53, tel: 011-261 8235; www.saran.co.rs.* A cut above, this Zemun institution is without question the best place in Belgrade to try traditional Serbian fish dishes. The food is outstanding, the service impeccable, and the ambience upmarket without being oppressive. The extravagant may choose to order an entire fish (perch, trout, sturgeon); otherwise, you could go a long way (or at least as far as Croatia's Adriatic coast) without finding such a delectable seafood risotto. Note that the name is given only in Cyrillic on the frontage: *Шаран*. Tues–Sun noon–1am.

TRAVEL ESSENTIALS

PRACTICAL INFORMATION

A

ACCOMMODATION

English is universally well-spoken in hotels, B&Bs and hostels. Pricing (in hotels and hostels alike) fluctuates based on season and occupancy; the concept of low/high seasons doesn't significantly affect pricing, as spring and autumn are as busy as the summer. Many hotels or hostels will give a discount (and an extra, such as a free drink on arrival) if you book directly through their website, instead of through a third-party aggregator. Wi-fi is standard in all accommodation; not all hotels offer free water or hairdryers. Homestay options (*sobe*) are available via the Tourist Office of Belgrade.

Do you have any rooms available? **Imate li slobodnih soba?**
A room for one/two **jednokrevetna/dvokrevetna soba**
What's the price per night? **Kolika je cena po noći?**
Is … breakfast included? **Da li su uključeni … doručak?**
What time is check-in/check-out? **U koliko sati je
    prijava/odjava?**

AIRPORTS

Nikola Tesla Airport (BEG, tel: 011-209 4444; www.beg.aero/eng) is situated 18km west of central Belgrade. International flights arrive into Terminal 2. To get to the city centre, the cheapest option is to take bus no.72, which leaves outside Terminal 2 (from the Departures level) every 40 minutes, dropping off at Zeleni Venac (a stop by Brankov bridge, *Brankov most*, in the city centre): from there, it's a 15-minute walk to Trg Republike. Buy your ticket from the kiosk (costing 89 dinars) or from the driver (costing 150 dinars). Another option is the A1 minibus to Trg Slavija in the Vračar district, leaving from outside Terminal 2 every 30 minutes – tickets cost 300 dinars from the driver. Both run from 5am until midnight.

To ensure that you won't be overcharged on an airport taxi, go to the official 'TAXI-INFO' stand as you emerge from Customs into the Arrivals hall; they will print you a slip showing your agreed fixed fare (typically 1,400–1,800 dinars to the city centre); you take this out to the taxi rank and hand it to your driver.

B

BICYCLE RENTAL

You will see very few cyclists in the city centre. It is not an attractive (or necessarily safe) cycling destination without an experienced guide, and although the city authorities have laid out an increased number of cycle paths, they are not yet all joined up. The banks of the Sava and Danube rivers in New Belgrade, however, are well equipped with freshly laid-out, designated cycle paths; there is also a cycle route around Ada Ciganlija. **iBikeBelgrade** (*Karadjordjeva 11*, tel: 066-900 8386; www.ibikebelgrade.com), founded by a Dutch cycling enthusiast, provides reliable bike hire for €10/day or €2.50/hour. English spoken; tandems, trailers and ebikes available.

BUDGETING FOR YOUR TRIP

Direct flights from the UK (London–Belgrade) are currently served by two operators: Wizz Air from London Luton (costing around €150–250 return) or Air Serbia from London Heathrow (around €230–350 return). From the US (NYC–Belgrade) flights with Air Serbia cost around €750–900; there are no direct flights from Australia. A train from the UK is not significantly cheaper than flying, but if preferred for environmental reasons, you will need to go via Paris, Munich and Zagreb, costing around €230 one-way.

Overall, living costs as a visitor to Belgrade are significantly lower than in the UK, US or Western capitals. Four-star hotels, B&Bs and chic design hostels are all significantly more affordable than in comparable European cities. A bed in a youth hostel dorm room will cost around €20–40 per night. A good-quality B&B, hotel or set of luxury rooms will cost from €70–120 for a double room with en-suite bathroom. Higher-end hotels start at around €140 for a double room.

Eating out is conspicuously affordable: breakfast or brunch, with an omelette, smoothie and coffee will cost no more than €8–10; a light lunch (one course and drinks) around €10–14; and a full evening meal in a high-quality, mid-range restaurant in the city centre around €25–35. Alcohol is affordable too, a beer typically costing around €2–3 and a cocktail around €4–5; coffees are around €1–2.50. Museum tickets cost around €2–5, with discounts of up to 50 percent for students presenting an ISIC (International Student Identity Card).

If travelling on a budget, stay at hostels and shop at a *pekara* (bakery) for cheap, filling breaded goods or *burek* and the open-air markets for fruit, vegetables and fresh foods. At many hotels, opt out of breakfast to save around €10.

C

CAR HIRE

Due to congestion, poor availability of parking, and hectic driving conditions, you are unlikely to want to hire a car to see central Belgrade. However, if you are including Belgrade in a tour of Serbia or the region, all the major car rental operators have a presence at Nikola Tesla Airport, including:

Auto-Rent tel: 063-349 341; www.carrental.co.rs
Avis tel: 011-209 7062; www.avis.rs
Europcar tel: 011-785 2820; www.europcar.rs

I'd like to rent a car. **Želim da iznajmim kola**
for …. days **na …. dana**
With basic (third-party)/full (comprehensive) insurance **Sa osnovnim/potpunim osiguranjem**
Fill it up with petrol/diesel, please **Napunite ga benzinom/ dizelom, molim**
The car's broken down **Kola se pokvario**
There's been an accident **Imali smo nesreću**

Hertz tel: 011-228 6017; www.hertz.rs
Sixt tel: 011-228 6356; www.sixt.rs

Car hire costs around €30–50 per day. When hiring a car, you will need to show a valid EU or international driving permit and to pay a sizeable deposit. Keep the vehicle registration documents with you at all times, and if you are involved in an accident get a European accident claim form, which you can present to the hire company and/or your insurer.

CHILDREN, TRAVELLING WITH

Baby change is not widely available, but is provided at the Rajićeva shopping centre (see page 95) on Knez Mihailova, at Nikola Tesla Airport, and in Red Bread café in Dorćol (see page 108). Generally, supermarkets and pharmacies are well stocked with baby food, wipes, nappies, cups and cutlery. It is common to see toddlers in buggies and older school-age children out with their parents in the evening.

CLIMATE

Belgrade has a temperate continental climate, with hot summers and pleasant, warm springs and autumns. Spring and autumn are popular times to visit; summer in the city brings temperatures in the high 20s°C (70s°F) that feel hotter, due to traffic fumes. The winter is relatively mild, with snowfall starting in November and clearing in March.

Monthly average temperatures are as follows:

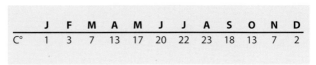

	J	F	M	A	M	J	J	A	S	O	N	D
C°	1	3	7	13	17	20	22	23	18	13	7	2

CLOTHING

You should be respectfully dressed when visiting churches; some, though not all, women will cover their heads with a headscarf.

CRIME AND SAFETY

You should take the same precautions here as in any major city, particularly late at night, as many bars and clubs are located in poorly lit streets, alleyways and apartment blocks. Be alert on public transport, around the main train and bus stations, in open-air markets and in subways. Be vigilant if attending (or in the vicinity of) large sporting events, which can become violent. If you are a victim of crime, report it to the police (192), or use the all-purpose emergency number (112). Note that English may not be spoken, and the 112 number runs an automated message in Serbian only; get a friendly Serbian-speaker to help.

D

DISABILITIES, TRAVELLERS WITH

Belgrade is, unfortunately, not generally well adapted for travellers with disabilities. Pavements and roads are often rutted and uneven, and only a very small number of bus/tram lines have wheelchair access (none running useful city-centre routes). However, a growing number of museums and cultural sites provide ramps for disabled access. Nikola Tesla Airport is fully adapted to travellers with disabilities. In the city centre, Rajićeva shopping centre offers disabled toilets.

DRIVING

In Serbia, you need to drive on the right, give way to traffic on the left, and overtake on the left. Speed limits are typically 120kmph on motorways, 100 kmph on dual carriageways and 50 kmph in built-up areas. Key rules to be aware of when driving: seatbelts are a legal requirement; no mobile phone use while driving; no children under 12 in the front; and dipped headlights must be used in all conditions. You are legally obliged to carry a reflective triangle, first-aid kit and other rescue equipment in your car (full list available online via the AA). If you are involved in an accident, call the Traffic Police on 192 or the all-Europe emergency number on 112 (English may not be spoken). If a hire car breaks down, contact the hire company.

In Belgrade, central car parks will allow you to stay for several hours (unlike the restrictive on-street parking system within the city centre): most convenient for the Old Town are the car parks on Obilićev venac or on Kraljice Natalice, near Terazije. Outside Belgrade, most major roads are free, but there are tolls on motorways such as the A1/E75 from Subotica to Novi Sad, Belgrade and Niš. Road conditions in the countryside are often poor.

E

ELECTRICITY
Standard European two-pin plugs are used (so you can use a Europe-wide adaptor). The standard voltage is 230V.

EMBASSIES AND CONSULATES
Australia: *Vladimira Popovića 38-40*, tel: 011-330 3400;
www.serbia.embassy.gov.au
Canada: *Kneza Miloša 75*, tel: 011-306 3000;
www.canadainternational.gc.ca/serbia-serbie
France: *Pariska 11*, tel: 011-302 3500
New Zealand: (consular issues for Serbia are handled from the Embassy in Rome, Italy): tel: (00) 64 99 20 20 20; www.mfat.govt.nz
South Africa: (consular issues for Serbia are handled from the Embassy in Sofia, Bulgaria): tel: (00) 359 2939 5015; www.dirco.gov.za/sofia
UK: *Resavska 46*, tel: 011-306 0900;
www.gov.uk/world/organisations/british-embassy-belgrade
US: *Bulevar kneza Aleksandra Karadjordjevića 92*, tel: 011-706 4000;
www.rs.usembassy.gov

I want to talk to … the American/Australian/British/Canadian embassy/consulate **Želim da razgovaram s … američkom/ australijskom/britanskom/kanadskom ambasadom/ konzulatom**

EMERGENCIES

In an emergency, call 192 (for the police), 194 (for an ambulance), 193 (the fire services) or 112 for the all-purpose emergency number. Note that English may not be spoken, and the 112 number runs an automated message in Serbian only; get a friendly Serbian-speaker to help.

F

FURTHER READING

For readers interested to delve deeper into Serbian history and culture, the following titles are strongly recommended:

Snippets of Serbia, Emma Fick (2015). An illustrated journey through Serbia by a young American artist living as an expat in Belgrade.

The Serbs: History, Myth and the Destruction of Yugoslavia, Tim Judah (2009). A thoughtful, readable account of modern Serbian history, told through the prism of the author's personal experiences as a journalist covering the wars of the 1990s.

The Balkans, 1804–2011: Nationalism, War and the Great Powers, Misha Glenny (2012). Magisterial account of contemporary Balkan history written by a former BBC correspondent.

Black Lamb and Grey Falcon: A Journey Through Yugoslavia, Rebecca West (1942). Classic account of pre-war travels through the interwar Kingdom of Yugoslavia, written beautifully by one of the twentieth-century's greatest travel writers.

Eastern Approaches, Fitzroy Maclean (1949). An action-packed account of Maclean's experiences in Yugoslavia during World War II as Churchill's wartime envoy to Tito's Partisans.

G

GETTING THERE

Flights: Direct flights from the UK (London airports) are available from Wizz Air (www.wizzair.com) from London Luton (around €150–250 return) or Air

Serbia (www.airserbia.com) from London Heathrow (around €230–350 return). London–Belgrade takes around 2hr 40min. EasyJet and Ryanair fly to Belgrade only indirectly via other European capitals. Air Serbia – formerly JAT, the Yugoslav national airline – also flies direct from NYC (JFK), taking 8hr 30min–10hr, and costing around €750–900 return. No direct flights operate from Australia; the easiest route is with Etihad (www.etihad.com) via Abu Dhabi (approx 23hr). Air Serbia flies direct to Belgrade from a wide range of European destinations such as Zurich, Frankfurt, Berlin and Moscow.

Bus: Belgrade Central Bus Station (*Beogradska autobuska stanica*, Železnička 4, tel: 011-263 6299) is around a 15min walk from Kalemegdan Fortress. Eurolines, operated in Serbia by Lašta, is the biggest single operator running international buses to and from Belgrade (*Železnička 2*, tel: 011-263 6299; www.lasta.rs), but as there are multiple operators, by far the best place to find up-to-date information on international bus and train timetables and pricing (and to book tickets) is the Polazak site (www.polazak.rs), which has an English version and aggregates information on all operators.

Options for bus routes across Europe include coming from Vienna (8hr 40min, costing around €30), Budapest (6hr, around €20), Zagreb (6hr, around €25) or Sarajevo (7–8hr, around €25). Note restrictions on travelling from Kosovo: it's possible to travel from Serbia into Kosovo and back again (as long as the return journey is within three months), but you are likely to have difficulties entering Serbia from Kosovo if your passport shows you entered Kosovo directly from anywhere else other than Serbia. (See also *Visas*.)

Train: The national rail company is Srbija Voz (www.srbvoz.rs/en). Trains are generally slower and much less reliable than buses in this region, often subject to several hours' delay. To add to the inconvenience, since July 2018, Belgrade's former main railway station is closed and all international trains run to and from **Belgrade Centre (Beograd Centar) railway station**, which has been under periodic construction since 1977 and is located further out of town, at Prokupačka ulica (*Savski venac*, tel: 011-397 5533). The station is often locally called Prokop. Facilities are still limited but its development continues, theoretically slated to complete by the end of 2023. For timetables, visit the Srbija Voz website (www.srbvoz.rs/en) or the Polazak aggregator (www.polazak.rs). Beograd Centar is not well connected to the city: pre-book a taxi, or take bus 36, which runs a circular route linking Beograd Centar and the old station nearer the old town. Avoid the taxis waiting outside, which will over-charge for a ride to the city centre.

The main international train routes link Belgrade to Sofia (vis Niš), Budapest (via Novi Sad and Subotica) and Zagreb. One famed route worth the effort is the beautiful Belgrade to Bar route (11–12hr, €20–25), passing through Pod-gorica and terminating in Bar on the Montenegrin coast. It's a marvel of en-gineering, with 254 tunnels and 435 bridges on the journey. Construction of the line started in the 1950s but only completed in 1976, opened by President Tito himself. To travel all the way to Belgrade from London, you need to leave London mid-morning, travelling to Paris via Eurostar, take the TGV to Munich and then overnight to either Zagreb or Budapest, and arrive in Belgrade by early evening the next day (see www.seat61.com/serbia).

GUIDES AND TOURS

The Tourist Organization of Belgrade (TOB) runs a range of city tours: book at the main tourist information office at Knez Mihailova 5. These include places on open-top bus tours, free walking tours or themed tours such as the Bel-grade beer tour. Between April and November, TOB can arrange your visit to the Royal Compound at Dedinje; they are group visits lasting two hours (cur-rently on hold due to the Covid-19 pandemic). Free daily walking tours from Belgrade Walking Tours (www.belgradewalkingtours.com, www.belgrade-freetour.com), including a downtown route and a twentieth-century history theme, start from Trg Republike at set times daily throughout the year.

iBikeBelgrade (*Karadjordjeva 11*, tel: 066-900 8386; www.ibikebelgrade. com) offers 3–4hr bike tours (many of them in English) between May and

Is there an English-speaking guide/an English interpreter? **Postoji li vodič za engleski jezik/prevodilac engleskog jezika?**

October, taking in the main sights of the city or (if preferred) focused on the Brutalist architecture of New Belgrade. YugoTours (tel: 066-801 8614; www. yugotour.com) offers excellent tours around the iconic sites of New Belgrade inside an old Zastava/Yugo car, particularly worthwhile as these are widely dispersed and not easy to walk to independently. This is also one of the best ways to (sensitively) visit Staro Sajmište concentration camp. Tours start from the iBikeBelgrade shop (*Karadjordjeva 11*).

H

HEALTH AND MEDICAL CARE

Tap water in Belgrade is safe to drink. Pharmacies carry a green cross sign; 24-hour pharmacies include Prima Pharmacy (*Francuska 37a*) and Prvi May (*Kralja Milana 9*). You should have comprehensive health and travel insurance before travelling to Serbia. Consult your travel clinic in good time before you travel, and check for up-to-date guidance on the TravelHealthPro website under Serbia country information (www.travelhealthpro.org.uk). The vaccinations currently advised for some travellers are Hepatitis A (if travelling in remote rural areas), Hepatitis B (as Serbia is a medium-high risk country, with two percent of the population thought to be infected) and rabies (as it has been reported in some domestic animals, bats may carry the virus). It is also worth being aware of the risk of tick-borne encephalitis in rural Serbia.

I don't feel well **Bolestan sam** (m.) **Bolesna sam** (f.)
I need ... a doctor/dentist/ambulance **Treba mi ... doctor/
    zubar/ambulantna kola**
I have ... an upset stomach/sunburn/a fever/toothache **Imam ...
    znemiren stomak/opekotina/groznica/zubobolja**
Where's the nearest (all night) pharmacy? **Gde je najbliža
    (noćna) apoteka?**

Due to Covid-19, countries may change entry requirements and close their borders at very short notice. Always check the Foreign, Commonwealth & Development Office (FCDO) website (www.gov.uk) and their specific country pages for the latest testing and vaccination requirements.

L

LANGUAGE

Serbian is a regional variant of the language formerly known as Serbo-Croat. The form of the Latin alphabet used in Serbia, Croatia, and Bosnia called 'Gaj's Latin alphabet' and includes a few special characters: **ć** as in church; **č** as in chalk (a slightly harsher 'ch' sound); **đ** or dj, as in gin (for ease of understanding, we have used the transliteration 'dj' throughout this guide); **lj** as in million; **nj** as in onion, **š** as in shut, and **ž** as in pleasure. Letters which are pronounced

Useful words and phrases
The basics
Yes **Da**
No **Ne**
0 **Nula**
1 **Jedan**
2 **Dva**
3 **Tri**
4 **Četiri**
5 **Pet**
6 **Šest**
7 **Sedam**
8 **Osam**
9 **Devet**
10 **Deset**

Hello (polite) **Dobar dan**
Hello (informal) **Zdravo**
Good morning **Dobro jutro**
Good evening **Dobro veče**
Good night! **Laku noć!**
Goodbye **Doviđenja** (the 'đ' sound is pronounced 'dj')
Bye **Zdravo**
Thank you/thank you very much **Hvala/mnogo vam hvala**
You're welcome **Molim**
Excuse me (*getting attention*) **Izvinite**
Can you help me? **Možeš li da mi pomogneš?**
Please **Molim**
Please may I have… **Mogu li da imam …**
I'm sorry (*apologizing*) **Izvinite**
Help! **Upomoć!**
Do you speak English? **Govorite li engleski?**
How are you? **Kako ste?**
I'm fine, thanks **Dobro, hvala**
What's your name? **Kako se zovete?**
My name's… **Zovem se...**
Nice to meet you **Drago mi je**
Where are you from? **Odakle si?**
I'm from the UK/the USA/Canada/Australia **Ja sam iz Velike
    Britanije/SAD/Kanade/Australije**
When? **Sada?**
Where? **Gde?**
Cheers! **Živeli!**
Have a nice day (or enjoy your meal)! **Prijatno!**
How much is it? **Koliko košta?**

differently to English are **c** (pronounced *ts* as in bi*t*s) and **j** (pronounced *y* as in *y*ou). English is widely spoken in hotels, restaurants, bars and clubs, but you will likely need to summon a few words of Serbian for taxis, public transport, kiosks, markets and shops.

Signs and notices
Otvoreno ОТВОРЕНО Open
Zatvoreno ЗАТВОРЕНО Closed
Ulaz УЛАЗ Entrance
Izlaz ИЗЛАЗ Exit
Guraj ГУРАЈ Push
Vuci ВУЦИ Pull
Zabranjeno ЗАБРАЊЕНО Forbidden
Opasnost ОПАСНОСТ Danger
Policija ПОЛИЦИЈА Police
Autobuske stanice АУТОБУСКЕ СТАНИЦЕ Bus station
Železničke stanice ЖЕЛЕЗНИЧКЕ СТАНИЦЕ Railway station
Taksi ТАКСИ Taxi

LGBTQ+ TRAVELLERS

Belgrade's LGBTQ+ scene remains relatively small and discreet. Pride events have historically been the focus of far-right attacks; since 2014 they have taken place with police protection, and been better attended. In 2017, Ana Brnabić became Prime Minister, making her only the second LGBTQ+ head of government in the world. However, even though all issues related to the LGBTQ+ community have improved, visitors should be aware that public prejudice against homosexuality and the LGBTQ population is still relatively high and public displays of affection may attract negative attention. The best place to obtain support or up-to-date information on what's on is the **Pride Info Centre** (*Prajd Info Centar, Kralja Milana 20*; Sun–Thurs 4pm–2am, Fri & Sat till 5am; www.parada.rs). One of the most central and long-established gay-friendly clubs/bars is **ClubMusk** (*Makedonska 28*; Sun–Thurs 4pm–2am, Fri & Sat till 5am; www.facebook.com/ClubMuskBelgrade).

M

MAPS

The Tourist Organization of Belgrade (TOB) at both Nikola Tesla airport and Knez Mihailova can provide a city map, covering both the centre and outlying areas, and with key bus routes marked. The PlanPlus maps online (www.PlanPlus.rs) give a greater level of detail and can be printed for free. For something more in-depth, order the Belgrade City Map from Magic Map (www.magicmap.rs).

MEDIA

There are no English-language listings magazines or newspapers in Belgrade. The most notable print outlets are the respected broadsheets *Politika* and *Danas*. Radio-Television Serbia (RTS) runs three national free-to-air TV channels. Radio station B92 (now online only at www.b92.net) was for many years a bastion of independent reporting, famously opposing Milošević in the 1990s.

MONEY

The Serbian currency is the dinar, abbreviated as din or RSD (Republic of Serbia Dinar). Dinars come in 1000, 500, 200, 100, 50, 20, and 10 notes; and 20, 10, 5, 2 and 1-dinar coins. You can also pay for accommodation (and sometimes meals) using euros. ATMs are the easiest place to withdraw currency (dinar or euros); a bank of ATMs await you in the Nikola Tesla Airport baggage hall. Exchange points (*menjačnica*) are available across town.

N

NIGHTCLUBS

Mainstream clubs often do not advertise entry fees but at the more popular *splavovi* or Savamala clubs, tourists risk being scammed (such as being made to pay over the odds for entry, or for a table in a VIP area to guarantee entry). To be on the safe side, if you want to go to one of these more mainstream clubs and don't have Serbian friends to navigate your way in, you can use the well-respected, free Belgrade at Night service (tel: 062-337 700; www.belgradeatnight.com) to book a table; they also offer options to book (for a fee) a host who will take you around the city's clubs, organize transport and ensure everything goes smoothly. This will not be necessary if you head to the alternative, more casual bar/clubs, such as those in Cetinjska.

Many bars or clubs have no website and instead use their Facebook pages; these can be useful for information on gigs, DJs and events.

O

OPENING TIMES

Many shops in central Belgrade are open until 8–9pm. Food shops such as minimarts typically open 6am–10pm. Government offices and banks are usually open Mon–Fri only (or *radnim dinom*, working days); government offices usually 8am–3/4pm, banks 9am–4/5pm. Many museums and cultural attractions are closed on Mondays. Many museums have late opening (8pm) one or more nights a week.

P

POLICE

Police in Belgrade wear dark blue uniforms with the word ПОЛИЦИЈА (*Policija*) on the back in Cyrillic; police cars are white with a dark blue stripe.

Where's the police station? **Gde je policijska stanica?**
I've lost my wallet/bag/passport/key/credit card **Izgubilo** (m.)/
Izgubila (f.) **... sam novčanik/torbu/pasoš/ključ/
kreditna kartica**

POST OFFICES

Post boxes are yellow. Post offices are marked Пошта (*Pošta*) with blue and yellow branding, and are usually open Mon–Sat 8am–7pm. The main post office is on Takovska 2, near the Parliament Building.

Where's the nearest post office? **Gde je najbliža pošta?**
Postage stamps **Poštanskih markica**

PUBLIC HOLIDAYS

New Year's Day holiday 1-2 January
Orthodox Christmas Day 7 January
Statehood Day 15-16 February
Orthodox Good Friday, Easter Sunday and Easter Monday April–May, variable: up to five weeks later than the Gregorian (western) church calendar
Labour Day 1-2 May
Armistice Day 11 November

R

RELIGION

Around 85 percent of the population of Serbia are Orthodox Christians, five percent Catholic and three percent Muslim. Whilst many people are not strictly observant, Orthodoxy is an important cultural force.

T

TELEPHONES

To dial out of Serbia to another country, you need to dial 00 followed by the country code (for example, 44 for the UK). To call a landline in Serbia from abroad, dial 00 then the country code, 381, followed by the Belgrade city code, 11. To dial a Belgrade number from inside Serbia, simply dial 011 and then a six- or seven-digit number. If calling from an overseas mobile, you will need to use the full country and city code (i.e. 00381 11) followed by the six- or seven-digit number. If you are calling a Serbian mobile number, the number will start with a code ranging from (060) through to (069), followed by a six or seven-digit mobile number. Several of the contact details for bars, cafés and restaurants given in this guide are for mobile numbers.

Serbia is not part of European Union roaming arrangements; to avoid roaming charges, you may want to consider getting a local SIM card for your phone, or a specific data plan from your mobile phone provider. It is possible to buy a local SIM card on arrival at Nikola Tesla Airport (in the baggage collection hall), such as the MTS Tourist SIM Card, priced at around €15 (120 minutes on local network and 10GB of internet over 30 days); however, this will not work if your phone is locked by your network.

TIME ZONES
Belgrade operates on a time zone one hour ahead of GMT in the winter, two hours ahead of GMT in the summer. This time zone chart shows local time in Belgrade versus international destinations during late spring/summer, when daylight saving is in place.

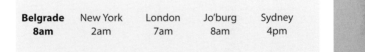

Belgrade	New York	London	Jo'burg	Sydney
8am	2am	7am	8am	4pm

TIPPING
Tipping (pleasingly called *bakšiš*) is normal, but not expected as routine. In taxis, the norm is to round up the bill to the nearest hundred dinars. Table service is still the norm in most cafés and bars, as well as restaurants, and service charges are not usually added to bills, leaving you with the discretion to tip when you pay the bill; 10–15 percent is usual. If you're in a rush, it

is considered perfectly polite to go up to the cash register to pay instead of waiting at your table.

TOILETS

Toilets are marked with the sign ТОАЛЕТ or TOALET. Male toilets are marked with the sign 'M', МУШКАРЦИ or MUŠKARCI; female toilets with the sign Ж, ЖЕНЕ or ŽENE. Toilets in the hotels and restaurants listed here will be clean and pleasant. Toilets in clubs, bars and museums or tourist sights are highly variable in cleanliness.

TOURIST INFORMATION

The Tourist Organization of Belgrade (TOB), which is responsible for tourism in the city, is separate from the Tourist Organisation of Serbia (TOS), which covers the rest of the country. English is spoken at both centres. TOB is most relevant for your time in Belgrade; its main branch is at Knez Mihailova 5, in the Belgrade City Library building (tel: 011-263 5622; www.tob.rs; email: bginfo@knezmihailova.tob.rs; Mon–Sat 9am–9pm, Sun 10am–3pm), with city maps, accommodation information and the usual guides/leaflets about tourist attractions. A secondary branch of TOB is located at Nikola Tesla Airport (tel: 011-209 7828; daily 9am–9.30pm) and offers orientation, maps and information about onward transport.

The central information centre for the Tourist Organisation of Serbia (TOS) can be found at Trg Republike 5 (tel: 011-655 7100; Mon–Fri 10am–9pm, Sat & Sun till 6pm).

TRANSPORT

Many visitors will not opt to use public transport on a short trip to Belgrade, as most downtown distances are walkable and taxis are very affordable (see below). Construction of the controversial Belgrade Metro finally got underway in 2022 but is not expected to be complete until at least 2030. Meanwhile, city public transport is provided by a network of bus, tram and trolleybus lines operated by **GSP Beograd** (tel; 011-366 4000; www.gsp.co.rs), but several private bus operators also run on around 130 Belgrade city routes.

BusPlus smartcards (BusPlus *kartica*) are the most cost-effective way to get around on all city transport (buses, trams and trolleybuses). There are two options available: the first is a one-day card which expires after 24 hours, costs 290 dinars and is valid for unlimited rides (so are ideally suited to visitors in Belgrade for a short break), or a long-term card (costing 250 dinars) which can be charged with a chosen amount of credit, and then topped up as and when required.

BusPlus passes are sold at small kiosks (with a BusPlus tag) dotted around the city (the main brand is MojKiosk). When boarding the bus, tram or trolleybus, touch your prepaid pass to the digital reader near the door. Cards valid for one, three or five days can be purchased at kiosks for 40 dinars, after which you have to pay 89 dinars for every 90min ride.

Buses and trolleybuses crisscross Belgrade more systematically than any other form of public transport; particularly useful routes for tackling the longer distances you may wish to cross in the city are listed below.

From the airport to the city centre, minibus A1 to/from Trg Slavija or bus 72 to/from Brankov bridge, close to Zeleni Venac). (See *Airports*.)

From Zeleni Venac (the stop by Brankov bridge) **across the river to New Belgrade** (Ušće or Palata Srbija – Palace of Serbia stops). Both are near the *splavovi* and Museum of Contemporary Art. Buses 84 or 15.

From Zeleni Venac or New Belgrade (Ušće or Palata Srbija – Palace of Serbia – stops) **onward to Zemun,** bus 84 (get off at the Glavna stop, Ze-

I'd like to go to …. **Želim da idem u …**
A single/return ticket, please **Jedna/Povratna karta**
Does this … bus/tram/train go to …? **Ide li ovaj autobus/ tramvay/voz do …?**
Where is the bus stop/tram stop for …? **Gde je autobus/ tramvay/voz za …?**
How much is the fare to … ? **Koliko košta vožnja do …?**

mun's main street).

From Studentski Trg (Old Town) to Vračar, buses 19, 21 or 22.

From Trg Republike (Republic Square) to Ada Ciganlija, bus 37.

Tram lines, generally speaking, serve residential areas, but tram no.2 runs a scenic circular route around the Old Town, skirting the edge of Kalemegdan Park via Pariska, and including stops near to Skadarska, Tašmajdan and Karadjordjeva (in Savamala).

Taxis are affordable in Belgrade: meters typically start at around 165 dinars and the cost of a ride is normally about 60 dinars per kilometre in the daytime, 85 dinars per kilometre from 10pm–6am, on Sundays or public holidays. Most taxis accept cash only. It is always best to book your taxi ahead of a planned journey rather than try to hail one on the street (hotels or restaurants will gladly help). Genuine taxis have a working meter and a plastic sign with a specific company name (not a white sign just saying 'TAXI') on the roof. Reputable companies include:

Beotaxi tel: 011-241 5555; www.radiobeotaxi.co.rs

Lux tel: 011-303 3123; www.luxtaxi.rs

Pink tel: 011-635 5000; www.pinktaxi.info

Many young Belgraders use the local Uber equivalent, **CarGo**, available as an app (see www.appcargo.com), instead.

V

VISAS AND ENTRY REQUIREMENTS

Citizens of the UK, US, Ireland and other EU countries, Australia, New Zealand and Canada do not need visas to visit Serbia for up to 90 days; citizens of South Africa will need to apply for a short-term visa via the Embassy in Pretoria (costing approximately R1055). All visitors also need to be able to provide proof of sufficient funds (calculated as €50 per day of intended stay) on request; full entry requirements are listed on the Ministry of Foreign Affairs website (www.mfa.rs).

You are required to register with the local police within 24 hours of your arrival in Serbia; any formal accommodation such as a hostel or hotel will do this for you upon check-in (usually when they take your passport), but if you are staying in a private home, make sure you get registered. Be aware that you may be denied entry to Serbia if you have Republic of Kosovo stamps in your passport (from any prior trip), or if you entered Kosovo from anywhere other than Serbia itself.

W

WEBSITES AND INTERNET ACCESS

Useful English-language websites include:

www.balkaninsight.com Balkan Insight from the Balkan Investigative Reporting Network, providing detailed and impartial news and features on Balkan politics and society.

www.b92.net.eng English-language version of major Serbian news site.

www.tob.rs The official website of the Tourist Organization of Belgrade (TOB), filled with useful information and resources.

www.planplus.rs Detailed online city maps.

www.stillinbelgrade.com An insider's guide to what's hip and happening in the city, with up-to-date information on bars, clubs and the cutting-edge cultural scene.

Wi-fi is available in almost all central Belgrade cafés and bars (just ask in English for the wi-fi password). You may spot wi-fi benches with in-built charging points and wi-fi access in city parks, which can be handy for when you are out and about.

Can I use your phone? **Mogu li da telefoniram?**
Can I borrow a phone charger/adaptor? **Mogu li da pozajmim punjač za telefon/adapter?**
Do you have (free) WiFi? **Imate li (besplatan) Vifi?**
What's the password? **Koja je lozinka?**

WHERE TO STAY

The hotels, hostels, apartments and B&Bs listed below are divided by area. For a first stay in Belgrade, a location in the Old Town – near Trg Republike, Knez Mihailova, Studentski Trg or Dorćol – is recommended, whether for a hotel, hostel or set of luxury apartments. For a fuller Belgrade experience, don't overlook the charms of the hostels and apartments aboard the floating rafts, or *splavovi,* in New Belgrade. If travelling for business, options in Vračar may appeal, with a number of high-quality, affordable four-star hotels.

In the past decade or so, Belgrade has seen a welcome proliferation of characterful boutique hotels. Most are four-star, but by pan-European standards very affordable. Luxury apartments and boutique B&Bs can also be excellent options, and offer cost savings compared to hotels of comparable quality; those listed here stand out for their quality accommodation, service and location. Hotels with two–three star ratings are increasingly rare; generally, this rating reflects their age and standards. Five-star hotels still tend towards the global chains, with the notable exception of the small number of boutique options listed here.

We have used the following symbols to give a range for pricing of the accommodation options listed, assuming a standard double room per night. Note that pricing varies not so much by season here as by occupancy and day of the week.

€€€€€	**over 251 euros**
€€€€	**121–250 euros**
€€€	**61–120 euros**
€€	**41–60 euros**
€	**below 40 euros**

OLD TOWN

Balkan Soul Hostel € *Kosančićev venac 11a, tel: 060-660 0685;* www.balkan-soulhostel.com. An outstanding city-centre hostel, set in a historic mansion at the end of cobbled Kosančićev venac (as you head away from Kalemegdan). The design is smart and stylish, with six dorms (all mixed) equipped with chunky dark-wood bunks. Bathrooms are new and clean (if small). Friendly staff plus funky interiors make a stay here the natural counterpart to a weekend exploring Belgrade's nightlife.

Belgrade Art Hotel €€€ *Kneza Mihaila (Knez Mihailova) 27, tel: 011-331 2000; www.belgradearthotel.com.* With a plum location on the main shopping thoroughfare of the Old Town, this hotel offers clean rooms and a perfectly pleasant, if somewhat functional, design and atmosphere. Most guests are business travellers, and the hotel prides itself on its reliability (rooms are all designed to the same aesthetic). The first-floor café-breakfast room overlooking Knez Mihailova is light and airy.

Dominic Smart Luxury Suites Trg Republike €€ *Obilićev venac 30, tel: 011-411 2060; www.dominicstay.com. Dominic Smart Luxury Suites* combines central locations with high-quality, spacious rooms (think floor-to-ceiling mirrors, low lighting, glass-walled bathrooms and White Company toiletries) at affordable prices. This outpost offers the best location in the city, just a stone's throw from Trg Republike and the National Museum. Breakfast not included in the rate.

Hotel Museum €€€ *Čika Ljubina 3-5, tel: 011-402 2100; www.hotelmuseum. rs.* Relatively new to Belgrade's boutique hotel scene, this 50-room bolthole is certainly giving the others a run for their money, with its enviable location immediately behind the National Museum. Service is professional; decor contemporary and stylish. Executive suites offer balconies looking directly onto the cupolas crowning the museum – an exclusive view if ever there was one.

Mama Shelter €€€ *Knez Mihailova 54, tel: 011-333 3000; www.mamashel-ter.com.* One of a French chain squarely targeting millennials, the Belgrade *Mama Shelter* couldn't be better located, in the new Rajićeva mall overlooking Kalemegdan Park. Rooms are super-comfortable, with quirky design and smart bathrooms. The focus is largely on younger travellers in Belgrade for the nightlife, with a rooftop bar with panoramic views, swinging seats and table football; in-house DJ nights; and an unusually wide breakfast spread, including juice-your-own smoothies, gluten-free bread and chia pudding.

Le Petit Piaf €€€ *Skadarska 34, tel: 011-303 5252;* www.petitpiaf.com. A friendly little family-run hotel set right in the heart of the Old Town's Ska-darlija district. Expect a warm welcome, helpful staff and charmingly old-fashioned touches, such as fresh white tablecloths and attentive table service at breakfast, instead of the standard soulless buffet. Rooms are in good condition, with new bathrooms, though relatively simply furnished. The street outside does get noisy at night – the flip-side to the fabulously central location.

Smokvica Dorćol Bed and Breakfast €€€ *Gospodar Jovanova 45a, tel: 069-446 4002;* www.smokvica.rs. This well-kept B&B is situated in one of the most visually harmonious corners of Dorćol, right above the popular *Smokvica* bistro, which also has a spacious stone courtyard. The pleasant, garret-style rooms are furnished with an eye to French country chic – think exposed beams, pastel-blue walls and geometric tiling. A great alternative to the larger hotels, with easy access to Dorćol's clutch of bars and boutiques. Free welcome drink.

Square Nine €€€€€ *Studentski Trg, tel: 011-333 3500;* www.squarenine.rs. A boutique five-star hotel designed by Brazilian architect Isay Weinfeld, *Square Nine*'s take on contemporary luxury blows the competition out of the water. The atmosphere throughout is one of hushed enjoyment, privacy and dis-cretion, with muted lighting, tasteful decor and carefully curated vintage and antique pieces. The lobby bar area is dotted with pieces of interest, from illuminated globes to a gigantic rug made from a patchwork of old Turkish *kilims*. Rooms feature cool bespoke furniture made in Denmark. The finish-ing touches: a rooftop Japanese restaurant and an 18m- (59ft-) long pool with spa.

Townhouse 27 €€€€ *Maršala Birjuzova 56, tel: 011-202 2900;* www.town-house27.com. One of the longest-established boutique hotels on the Belgrade scene, *Townhouse 27* stands out for its excellent location on pe-destrianized Topličin Venac and its thoughtful, personal service. Set in a tall, narrow townhouse with a cluster of rooms on each floor, this lovely bolthole has a welcoming, homely feel. Rooms are sleek in style without compromis-ing on comfort. Artworks by local Belgrade artists are displayed on rotation in the corridors.

WIDER CITY CENTRE

88 Rooms €€€ *Takovska 49, tel: 011-411 9088;* www.88rooms.com. Located on the charmless and thrumming traffic arterial of Takovska, this hotel with – you guessed it – 88 rooms offers good value for money. It is, apparently, Southeastern Europe's first hotel designed on feng shui principles; gleaming black stone and dark wood feature heavily in the interiors. All rooms have soundproofed windows so you can rely on a good night's sleep. It is a fair old walk to get to the prettier parts of town, but the pricing reflects this. Family suites available. Rooftop restaurant.

Dominic Smart Luxury Suites Parliament €€ *Kosovska 39, tel: 011-411 2060;* www.dominicstay.com. The rooms and ambience here match the high quality of the other two *Dominic* locations, with luxurious bedding and towels, subtle lighting and brand-new bathrooms. It's a snip at the price, and well worth considering if you are happy to venture away from the standard hotel format. On the fourth floor of a residential/business block, the Parliament site offers views onto the back of the National Assembly, and is close to St Mark's Church and Tašmajdan. Breakfast not offered, but water, tea and coffee are free.

Dominic Smart Luxury Suites Terazije €€ *Terazije 12, tel: 011-411 2060;* www.dominicstay.com. On the major thoroughfare cutting through the commercial district downtown, this branch of *Dominic Smart Luxury Suites* was the original and matches the others listed here for the very high quality of accommodation offered. Expect all the advantages of a four-star hotel (except an on-site restaurant) at budget-friendly prices in extremely convenient central locations.

Heritage Belgrade Garni €€€ *Mije Kovacevic 7A, tel: 11-715 1060;* www.heritagebelgrade.com/en. Located on one of the main streets in Belgrade within walking distance of the city centre, this four-star hotel comprises 40 modern and spacious rooms and suites, all tastefully decorated. Parking is available to guests at no extra charge, and an airport shuttle is provided for further convenience. On the ninth floor is an open-air gastro bar with panoramic city views. A little outside the heart of Belgrade but the good-value accommodation reflects this.

Hotel Mint €€ *Kvarnerska 4, tel: 11-411 3311*; www.hotelmint.rs. Family owned, this attractive white abode offers a perfect blend of contemporary style and traditional cosiness. Service is provided with a personal touch characteristic of Serbian hospitality. Each morning the breakfast buffet tempts with delicious homemade food. All the bedrooms are spacious and elegantly designed. The hotel is located in a quiet area filled with parks, villas and some of the better-kept Belgrade secrets, just a pleasant walk to the city centre, or five minutes by taxi.

Hotel Moskva €€€€ *Balkanska 1, tel: 011-364 2069;* www.hotelmoskva.rs. The 1908 Secessionist building, situated at the corner of Terazije and Balkanska, is a Belgrade landmark. The curved entranceway with its red carpet and rotating doors, just behind the Miloš Obrenović fountain on Terazije, nods to grandeur and prestige. Rooms have a relatively old-fashioned aesthetic, more sumptuous sparkle than minimalist monotones; the building has protected status, and renovations are thus limited. The spa (sauna, hammam, whirlpool – no pool) is sparkling white and state of the art, however. The lobby café is a refined spot for coffee and cakes (a tad overpriced, but undeniably delicious).

VRAČAR

Argo €€€ *Kralja Milana 25, tel: 011-364 0425;* www.argohotelbelgrade.com. A small 20-room hotel on the main drag in Vračar heading down towards St. Sava's Church, just opposite the famous Beogradjanka ('Belgrade lady') tower block. *Argo's* exceptionally friendly and helpful staff is its real USP, going out of their way to create a welcoming atmosphere. Rooms (twin, double and family) are cheerfully decorated, fresh and clean and soundproofed – useful given the location.

Crystal Hotel €€€ *Internacionalnih Brigada 9, tel: 011-715 1000;* www.crystal-hotel-belgrade.rs. A friendly, low-key four-star hotel popular with business travellers, situated on a quiet street in the leafiest part of Vračar, just minutes' walk from St Sava's Church. With 35 rooms and family-friendly suites, its crowning glory is its rooftop bar with 360-degree glass surrounds (appropriately enough, named 'the View'). The style throughout is a touch eclectic, but modern.

Hotel Tesla €€€ *Sumatovacka 42, tel: 011-243 0322;* www.hoteltesla.rs. A modern, four-star design hotel drawing inspiration from Serbia's most famous scientist. The 17 stylish and space-savvy rooms of this urban bolthole cleverly pay homage to Tesla through sepia wall murals of the man himself along with illustrations of his inventions. Many have outdoor terraces; all have extra-long beds – the legacy of the former professional basketball player on the team behind the hotel. Just a 20min walk to the Nikola Tesla Museum, which is free to guests.

Mark Hotel €€€ *Resavska 29, tel: 011-334 5400;* www.markhotelbelgrade.com. A reliable, affordable hotel adorned with up-to-date decor (teal paint, gold highlighting and giant mirrors), situated just off the main street (Kralja Milana) in Vračar. Rooms and apartments are simple but comfortable, with modern bathrooms and power showers. A 15min walk up Kralja Milana to reach Trg Republike.

Marquise Hotel €€€ *Mišarska 6, tel: 011-411 7100;* www.marquisehotel.rs. Tucked away on a pedestrianized passageway near Njegoševa, this delightful 25-room hideout is set in a 1905 building that once housed the city's public baths. It opened in 2018, following a sensitive redesign that integrates the building's history with stripped-back brickwork. Rooms are tastefully furnished in teal and cream. Underground bar/restaurant, where breakfast is served.

Saint 10 €€€€ *Svetog Save 10, tel: 011-411 6633;* www.saintten.com. Expect large, modern rooms and punctilious service at this five-star big-hitter on the approach to St Sava's on Vračar plateau. Rooms are well equipped for business travel, with desks, comfortable seating areas and glass-panelled bathrooms. Attention to detail is good, with towelling robes, complimentary minibar, espresso machines and free bike hire. All tastes are catered for at breakfast, with a range of healthy options (smoothies, salads, quinoa, fruit) as well as heartier fare (pancakes, *burek*, pork specialities, pastries).

SAVAMALA

Savamala Bed and Breakfast €€ *Kraljevića Marka 6, tel: 011-406 0264;* www.savamalahotel.rs. This on-trend B&B has the feel of a high-end hostel, with original artwork in the lobby area and workspace. Chic, spacious rooms have comfortable bedding and dark-tiled bathrooms. The location is perfect if you're primarily in Belgrade to party (with Savamala playing host to some of the city's biggest clubs); otherwise, it's a little out of town, and the area is rather mixed.

NEW BELGRADE

ArkaBarka €€ *Ušće bb, Blok 14, tel: 064-925 3507;* www.arkabarka.net. One of the longest-established and largest floating hostels on the Danube waterfront, *ArkaBarka* has glass panelling facing the river on three sides. A large, peaceful terrace suspends you just above the water, while a sociable, beach-bar style café is the perfect spot to linger over craft beers. Walk the wobbly plank from the walkway on the edge of Friendship Park. Snug single and double cabins or more spacious apartments offered on a second raft; family rooms and women-only dorms also available. Some added bonuses: generous breakfasts, two saunas and free bike rental for plying New Belgrade's riverside bike paths.

San Art €€ *Ušće bb, tel: 064-238 278;* www.sanarthostel.rs. This floating raft, close by *ArkaBarka*, offers a quieter atmosphere and more of a family feel than its popular neighbour. Older children will relish the experience of sleeping on the river as the raft bobs gently up and down on the water. Long-standing staff provide a warm and friendly welcome. Room furnishings and bedding are a touch old-fashioned, but comfortable and clean, with private bathrooms and air conditioning. Several rooms are suited to families staying in various configurations.

ZEMUN

Garni Hotel D10 €€ *Dobanovačka 10, tel: 011-400 3285;* www.hoteld10.com/en. This family-friendly hotel can be found in a peaceful corner of Zemun, a short hop from the shore of the Danube, with plenty of restaurants and bars within easy walking distance. Each of the 13 modern rooms is tastefully designed. The hosts are very friendly and go out of their way to make sure you are well fed from the diverse buffet breakfast served each morning. Complimentary bikes are provided for guest use so you can easily explore the city on two wheels.

INDEX

THE **MINI** ROUGH GUIDE TO
BELGRADE

First Edition 2022

Editor: Joanna Reeves
Author: Sophie Radford
Picture Editor: Tom Smyth
Cartography Update: Carte
Layout: Pradeep Thapliyal
Head of DTP and Pre-Press: Katie Bennett
Head of Publishing: Kate Drynan
Photography Credits: Alamy 4ML, 7T, 73, 86;
Getty Images 12, 17, 24, 27, 28, 29, 35, 92; iStock
1, 4TC, 4TC, 4TL, 5M, 5M, 6T, 6B, 7B, 18, 21, 22,
32, 34, 37, 38, 39, 40, 43, 44, 46, 48, 49, 50, 52,
54, 55, 57, 58, 59, 60, 64, 67, 72, 75, 79, 82, 94,
98, 103, 104; Natalija Milošević/Yugotour 4MC;
Shutterstock 4MC, 4ML, 5T, 10, 14, 36, 41, 47, 53,
62, 65, 68, 70, 74, 77, 81, 84, 87, 88, 90, 93, 97, 100
Cover Credits: Church of Saint Sava **miamia/
Shutterstock**

Distribution
UK, Ireland and Europe: Apa Publications (UK)
Ltd; sales@roughguides.com
United States and Canada: Ingram Publisher
Services; ips@ingramcontent.com
Australia and New Zealand: Booktopia;
retailer@booktopia.com.au
Worldwide: Apa Publications (UK) Ltd;
sales@roughguides.com

**Special Sales, Content Licensing
and CoPublishing**
Rough Guides can be purchased in bulk
quantities at discounted prices. We can create
special editions, personalised jackets and
corporate imprints tailored to your needs. sales@
roughguides.com; http://roughguides.com

Contact us
Every effort has been made to provide accurate
information in this publication, but changes
are inevitable. The publisher cannot be held
responsible for any resulting loss, inconvenience
or injury sustained by any traveller as a result
of information or advice contained in the
guide. We would appreciate it if readers would
call our attention to any errors or outdated
information, or if you feel we've left something
out. Please send your comments with the subject
line "Rough Guide Mini Belgrade Update" to
mail@uk.roughguides.com.